The Flight of
The Soul Millionaire

*For Radical Financial Advisers
Who Dare To Soar*

David J Scarlett

First Published in Great Britain in 2019 by Springtime Books

ISBN: 978-1-9997323-7-0

Cover and internal pages designed by Upshot
upshotdesign.co.uk

Praise for
The Flight of The Soul Millionaire

"I can't recall anything like this being written within the library of UK Financial Services books or reports. A fascinating lyricism weaving itself throughout a well-tested and transformational Journey.

David has a voice and a message which demands to be heard. I'm hooked on The Soul Millionaire Journey, and I love the allusion to 'Flight' throughout.

This book should be on the required reading list of every graduate who enters the financial planning profession."

Barry Horner
CEO Paradigm Norton and chair of the Financial Planning Standards Board

***

"There's no question in my mind that The Flight of The Soul Millionaire *shows you how to take your own flight to greatness.*

Elevating your thinking above the 'busy work' many entrepreneurs become entrenched in, David helps you to see what is really important, and then points the way to make your wildest dreams a reality.

Filled with tested principles, practical thinking exercises and inspiring stories, I defy anyone not to be transformed by the words of wisdom contained within this unusual book."

Matthew Smith, MSc, CFP™, MCSI, FPFS, IMC
Managing Director, Buckingham Gate Chartered Financial Planners

"I've read many books about financial planning, but it was a delight for me to be asked to review this one.

Not since the late, great Dick Wagner CFP™ put Financial Planners up there with the 3 great professions – Medicine, Law and Theology – have I seen the link to spirituality so clearly defined. The world will be a much better place with advisers putting this kind of proposition at the heart of what they do for clients. They'll be lifted upon the shoulders of their peers as heroes.

It's so fitting that at last someone has the courage to talk about the second most addressed topic in the bible in this way. Have you noticed how every single aspect of life is impacted by our poor relationships with money?

Read this and you'll make a hero's impact on the world, starting with your clients. Then they'll cheerfully pay your fees and introduce you to their family and friends."

**Sharon Sutton, Immediate Past President,
Chair UK Financial Planning Practitioner Panel, Personal Finance Society.
Managing Director, Thornton Chartered Financial Planners**

***

"Seven years ago, I encountered David's first book – The Soul Millionaire. *I was inspired then. I'm inspired again. But more so.*

This new work really delivers: the deconstruction of 'the old ways'; owning a purpose beyond profit; clear strategic direction; the reasons why clients will pay you much more; the art and science of coaching; the power to influence clients' lives for good; developing inspired leadership.
Then, the tools to give traction to all the above.

It's encouraging, exciting, even spiritual, stuff.

I urge you to read it. Read it again. Act on it. You'll change lives."

**Ruth Sturkey, FPFS Chartered Financial Planner CFP™,
Client Director – London, Paradigm Norton Financial Planning Ltd**

"Each chapter is beautifully written; the messages supported by persuasive logic and well-researched evidence.

Understanding the need for a passionate mission, the valuable ideas on change, the carefully curated processes and checklists... this cannot help but transform business results, team effectiveness and – most importantly – clients' lives."

Steve Gazzard, Director, S J Gazzard Consulting Ltd

***

"This is an exciting and, frankly, joy-inspiring book; dealing with a truly brave topic. A far, far cry from any other business book I have ever read, simply because it's about what actually matters.

It's not merely about doing; it's about feeling. It's about purpose and igniting something truly great.

If you have the fire in your belly to create something better. If you really want to make a difference, then this book just might change your life."

Philippa Hann, Partner, Clarke Willmott LLP

***

"The Soul Millionaire Journey that David has created achieves something quite extraordinary.
He lets you, intimately, into his world; while lifting your sights to horizons for your business you'd thought most unlikely.

What's more, I know from experience that David is the real deal. He has travelled this Journey himself.

In my experience, this book – and The Soul Millionaire Journey which it explains – can take you to places and accomplishments you never dreamed were possible."

Austyn Smith, Wealth Management Director, Austyn Smith Associates Ltd

"The world of retail financial services is at a crossroads right now; and this book has arrived at the perfect time. Through a truly engaging narrative, David takes the reader on a journey of self-discovery, and provides a clear roadmap for the way ahead for enlightened financial planners.

David is a master story teller, which ensures that the message gets through loud and clear. If you want to make a positive impact for your clients, do meaningful work and leave a legacy, this book is an essential read. As David says, 'Dare to be different, not just better'."

Alan Smith, CEO, Capital Asset Management

***

"This book – this unusual, inspirational, elevating book – has brought fresh breath to my dreams, magnified those dreams... and then given them wings!

Through it, I now see more clearly what success means. I see the business I want to build and lead; the greater impact I can have on others; the life I wish to embrace; the person I want to become. I've no doubt that the principles and frameworks within these pages will guide me to that future.

David's drive to lift, encourage and lead others is evident in every page of The Flight of The Soul Millionaire. *And the feeling is catching. I'm now convinced I can do precisely the same through my own business."*

Simon Glazier, Managing Director, Stewardship Wealth

***

"It's a rare gift: mixing fascinating stories worth listening to with structured, results-creating coaching in one book. No wonder some busy, stretched leaders in this profession have consumed its pages in just one or two sittings. Myself included!"

Jo Little FPFS, Chartered Financial Planner, Co-Founder, Eelah Ltd

"I knew – I just knew – from the very first pages, that this book was different.

It speaks to me in my language. It understands my desire to do great work and to serve selflessly. I hear my own words echoed back to me: "Imagine if businesses existed, not just to make shareholders richer, but to **really** make a difference!"

The journey that David so beautifully and clearly describes is about how to build that heart-centred business; one that has real purpose and truly delivers freedom. This is a blueprint for you to use, step by step, to bring your firm's vision to life. Work through it; keep it close; go back to it, again and again, for reference.

If you sense the transformative powers that are possible (not just for your clients, but for everyone it touches), when a financial planning business is founded on a purpose beyond profit... then this book is for you!"

**Tina Weeks, RLP, Financial Life Planner,
Director, Serenity Financial Planning Ltd**

***

*"Who wouldn't love to possess the power to change the world around us?
Who wouldn't love to develop a business capable of that kind of impact?*

Well, having travelled The Soul Millionaire Journey, I now see how that's entirely possible. I've certainly changed my world. So can you.

David's voice and message, taking you on this Journey, deserves to be heard."

Parminder Bains, Managing Director, Seasons of Wealth Ltd

***

"This business book succeeded in moving, inspiring, unsettling and motivating me!"

Margaret Mearns, Mearns and Company, Chartered Financial Planners

"Whether listening to David at a conference some years ago, or following the Journey outlined in this new book, David's message has constantly chimed with my own thoughts. It felt radical then. It does today.

The fact is, his candid views over the years have been very much at odds with the general consensus of this industry. That is what makes his message so attractive.
I have been the privileged beneficiary of that message, and that approach, since we first met.

David's profound desire to transform our industry into a true, highly-valued profession was apparent years ago. Now – in this opus – he captures principles and practices which can enable that transformation.

I urge you to read it."

Tim Sargisson, Chief Executive Officer, Sandringham Financial Partners

***

"Here are principles that make you think again, stories that captivate, examples that you can get your teeth into.

I challenge any author about to pen their Financial Services thoughts to come up with anything as fascinating, inspiring or original."

Andy McLaughlin, Managing Director, Astute Wealth Management Ltd

***

"What a brilliant book!

Not just because it's a superb read. More than that, it has started to shape my desire to really, really help people through our business. And has given me an empathetic way to energise them into action, to fulfil their dreams.

Our team's desire to make a difference in this way has been there for quite a while. But it has taken this book to make it come alive, to make it a reality."

Casey Mills, Managing Director, TFP Financial Planning Ltd

"The Flight of The Soul Millionaire *is a wonderful read. For those who are ready to begin The Soul Millionaire Journey described within it, you'll find that this book acts like your Business GPS.*

It will help you develop the type of business you dream of. It will help you become the person you were always meant to be. Ultimately, you'll become both the student and the hero in your own story!"

Mark A Smith, Partner, Simpsons Wealth Management

***

"*This is a brilliant book, packed with motivational real-life case studies.*

It offers you, the reader, a practical and step-by-step framework to establish a transformational financial planning practice, with a strong purpose and vision.

Highly readable and unique, this book will energise you, and inspire you to take action."

Dr Lien Luu, Associate Professor of Finance, University of Coventry

***

"*Meeting with David 10 years ago changed my life – in business, and personally. I believe this excellent book could have the same impact on you.*

His crucial and unusual skill is helping leaders to understand the Why (not just the What) in The Journey towards a Great Business.

This is a 'Must Read', if what you wish to do is to change lives – starting with yours. I urge you, most sincerely, to read it; and then try it for yourself."

Nigel Barker-Smith, Founder, NBS Financial Planning
UK Trainer for The Kinder Institute of Life Planning

"This book is a 'must read' for any Financial Planner – beginner or not – who is sincere in placing clients' interests above their own.

Yes, I believe that – like me – you'll find the stories inspirational, and will be captivated by the way David tells them.
And, I can assure you, they come alive when you meet the people themselves.

However, this is more than a book of inspiring stories. If you're wise, you'll use it as a reference book; because you'll learn from it every time you re-read it.

(David, if only you had been able to write this 30 years ago!)."

D James Martineau, CFP™ Chartered FCSI, Director, Lee Strathy Ltd

***

"The Flight of The Soul Millionaire is full of powerful ideas that will force you to question yourself, your life and the impact you have on the world around you.

If you want to experience something exceptional in the field of Financial Planning, then this book is for you. It will encourage and excite you to accomplish more than you probably thought possible!"

Stephen Buckle, Managing Director, Ashworth Financial Planning Ltd

***

"You're going to be surprised. I was.

David has distilled the essence of a series of real-life transformational business journeys; and created a thought-provoking package that can be digested in a day. But that is where the soul searching begins! Because he's showing you how to transform YOU; not just your business.

So, I encourage you to take the lessons of the book, and allow them to highlight your shortcomings. Then exercise the courage to change what you've learned... and so change the world around you.

Not everyone can handle that. That's why you'll be amongst a rare breed who will take the future with them."

Steve Hughes, Head of Compliance & Operations, Octagon Consultancy

For Wendy

You encourage me to soar.
You show me how to lift others.
You point the way to what really matters.

To soar. To lift. To matter.
This is what I yearn for. Because of you.

Contents

Acknowledgements

Throughout my life, there have been memorable individuals who have influenced my thinking, my behaviour and my perspective. When I was at a crossroads, in pain or joyful... they appeared.

I'm eternally grateful to them.

As practised as I'm becoming at crafting my thoughts and feelings into words, I'm not sure that I'm gifted enough to capture on this page just what they have meant to me in my life.

So, considering the creation of this book, there is one person who has worked, laboured and toiled with me through every sentence and phrase, every stage and step, every chapter and subheading.

It's Jo Parfitt. Editor and mentor extraordinaire.
She has helped to create order and sanity out of chaos and crazy ideas.

In parallel, she has also encouraged me to be emotionally and spiritually authentic when I become too mechanical or try to mimic others.

There were times when I silently – and openly – snarled and snapped, whinged and whined, mumbled and moaned at her, so demanding is she of excellence and the very best of me.

There were even times when I physically wanted to throw the manuscript at her, despite living in different countries.

In the face of all this she would soothingly say, *"I know you hate me. But you know I've got your back."* These words take the wind completely out of your sails, don't they?

Now here we are, with a book into which I've poured myself, over many hopeful months. And I feel gratified by what I see – perhaps what Jo could already see many months before.

Then there's the executive coach, teacher and minister Don McFarlane. That I even considered writing this book was his idea. At a point in my life where I had nestled into a comfortable routine, he shook me up, lifted me high, and helped me to see something magnificent that I'd yet to attempt.

In launching myself on this new venture, it's fair to say that both of us were influenced by entrepreneurs like Daniel Priestley; particularly his five-step approach to becoming a Key Person of Influence. Step #2 is *Publish.* And I can already see – as he suggests – how many products and services can flow from the coherent thinking demanded when writing a book like this.

I've also received great confidence, in writing boldly, because of the substantial research conducted by other consultants, speakers and authors such as Julie Littlechild (founder of Absolute Engagement) and Steve Wershing, CFP® (President of The Client Driven Practice LLC). Their work, both individually and together, has provided additional empirical evidence to support the reasons behind the years of success enjoyed by both myself and my clients.

However, having great ideas is one thing. Articulating those ideas in a coherent form is something else.

When I started writing, Wendy, my amazing wife, was right there to support this new crazy project (with no obvious reward). It's what she does; it's what she's always done.

Yet few could be tougher when it comes to critiquing my work. If Wendy says, *"Hmmm, this is fine,"* then I know I'm penning something quite brilliant!

Then there is my Mum and my Dad. Long before I thought I could write, they already let me know that whenever I did so, they would be the first ones to read it. They encouraged me that I was perfectly capable of doing better than them. Yet, what they have accomplished has been life-changing (and worth writing about in another book).

Of course, without the stories in here, this book would be dry and academic. Those stories, in various ways, include influences from each of our children: Adrian, Matthew, Lauren, Thomasina and Briony. They inspire me with their talents and courage.

And most of the stories wouldn't have been written at all without the wonderful tribe of clients I've worked with over the last 15 years: the Marys, the Simons, the Richards, the Andys, the Matthews, the Marks, the Rebeccas, the Steves, the Jos, the Alfies (well, just the one actually) and Satnam... you're all in here somewhere. You trusted me, and I was left breathless by what you accomplished, both during and after our work together.

As I scan the decades, I wish my English and German teachers, from Elliott Comprehensive in Putney, could see me now. They said that I could write, and I didn't believe them.

I'll show them the manuscript someday, when we meet again, years from now.

And we'll smile together at what is possible when others believe in you even more than you believe in yourself.

Foreword

If we think too long about how to ride the white-water rapids of change in the financial services landscape, we might end up immobilised by the sheer scale of what's ahead.

And yet, the possibilities we face are precisely what make this challenge so exhilarating.

What seems clear to me, as I survey the many questions facing us, is that we're privileged to be at a tipping point in history. This is the season when we can shape the way the financial services sector influences, and is regarded by, other professionals and, more importantly, the public we serve.

Which is why this book is so very timely.

Yes, financial advice and financial planning have evolved. Yet, I wonder just how many recognise how far this evolution could go? Or recognise how much better placed we are today to influence clients' lives, in addition to curating and caring for their money?

If we're to change the way the world views this profession, then we need to go beyond improving our technical expertise, beyond employing better tactics, techniques, technology and tools. Necessary as these are, taken alone, they are unlikely to have the impact we hope for.

What's more, I'm not sure that crafting new presentations, new marketing approaches or new ways of talking to clients will, by themselves, accomplish what's needed.

I believe what's needed is more profound than that. Perhaps what's needed is a shift beyond technical evolution. Could it be a root change in thinking, a breaking with tradition?

This last question illustrates why I think the book you have before you is so important. What is said here, and how it is explained, is sufficiently different as to be almost revolutionary.

There are three things that pique my interest in this book:

→ **Firstly**, it points out that, done well, the role of any financial advisory business is potentially transformative. And that, if everybody recognised this potential, many of us would no doubt behave differently, serve differently and be seen differently.

This change in approach, the book persuasively posits, would increase the public's trust, quickly and lastingly.

→ **Secondly**, the book presents a coherent, well-researched framework – The Soul Millionaire Journey – for any business that wishes to elevate its performance and influence.

Pointing to such readily-accessible, empirical evidence gives substance to the book's approach and messages. Guided by the book's framework, leaders can make a greater difference to their clients, whilst developing an inspirational culture for their team to thrive in.

→ **Thirdly**, I find that the book's unusual narrative provides a carefully-documented perspective which goes beyond the drive for short-term commercial results or instant gratification.

What you'll discover in these pages are the questions and answers that create better businesses – more sustainable, more richly fulfilling, more trusted and more enjoyable.

I've read many a book that talks about how things could be different.

However, following the stages of The Soul Millionaire Journey, I've been reassured by what happens when people actually do things completely differently. And what I've read is nothing if not different. I can find no other book that explains the process of business and success in quite the same way.

Finally, what emerges for me as being entirely different, is that this book, with its Journey, is not just about a firm's leader(s) changing their business model; this book is about the leader(s) changing themselves.

When we're prepared to change our minds, and change our behaviour, that, I believe, is the start of creating a great company – large or small.

I think you'll agree: we could all do with a few more great companies in our world today. And there's no reason why this profession cannot be in the vanguard of what is truly great.

Tim Sargisson, CEO, Sandringham Financial Partners

Preface

How to Use This Book

One of the great temptations in first scanning a book like this is that you'll fall into the *where's-the-attract-more-clients-and-make-more-money-section?* trap.

Please, don't fall for it.

There's a range of books out there that are perfectly adequate in showing you how to accomplish those things. I've read them. I've used them. I've found them extremely helpful throughout my career.

But if that knowledge is all you want...
Then this is not the book for you.

The coherent framework – the Journey – I've created here is designed to go well beyond clients and money. It's designed to create something significant, meaningful and hugely enjoyable – not to mention financially-propelling and freedom-creating.

Just like the construction of any framework, there are foundational stages that ensure power, reach, sustainability and scalability.

Avoid those stages, and you'll make money.
But you'll never be a transformative influence on your clients and your profession.
You'll never be a model that others would love to follow.
You'll never be iconic.

So, could you skip chapters and stages, and still benefit from what you read?

Yes, you could.

But is skipping stages likely to create a culture that others would be attracted to, relish being part of, and talk about freely and glowingly to others?

I don't believe so for a second.

And the research suggests that just focusing on finances would be taking a myopic approach to your stewardship, which should be about impacting the lives of others in areas of great importance to them.

There's an order to this enlightened impact.
There really is a step-by-step Journey to embark upon.
And each step has been tested, analysed and made accountable countless times.

Then there's what happens when you've concluded each chapter. At the end of each one you'll find an invitation to do three things:

→ **Firstly**, I'll invite you to read the concluding subchapter, *Come With Me to The Thinking Bench.*

Sit with me for a while, away from the hubbub of your life. Ponder the personal stories that I'll share with you here. Consider the messages that weave themselves through those stories.
Then map them across to your business, and to your life.

→ **Secondly**, I'll invite you to consider the subsection, *What Have You Learned?*

If you're like me, your first impulse will be to rush to the next chapter.
Yet, each chapter will become more relevant, more real, when you take each question and face your own business and personal life using that question as a lens.

→ **Thirdly**, join me as we get up close, nose-to-nose, and I ask you, *"What Will You Do Now?"*

None of what you're about to read will matter one jot or tittle in your life unless you're moved to action. Tangible results, which can comfortably be described as "astonishing", have been accomplished by those who have acted on each step of this Journey.

What that means is that the principles and practices, the strategies and practical steps, are not in question here – there's far too much evidence in the public domain for that.

The only matter in question is the capacity of each of us to see what is possible. Having seen that, then the next question concerns our willingness and commitment to at least experiment with this framework, this Journey.

If you do commit to taking the first baby steps, you'll inevitably find that something will change, and change for the better.

That change will be not just what you design and build. That change will be seen in who you become.

So, take a chance on becoming somebody others will be influenced and elevated by.

Join me on The Soul Millionaire Journey!

Introduction

"But they... shall renew their strength;
they shall mount up with wings as eagles;
they shall run, and not be weary; and they
shall walk, and not faint."

Isaiah 40:31

I would wake up, gasping for breath, my heart beating wildly.

I would glance feverishly around the room, at the walls and
the ceiling... and wonder if I could do it this time...

Wonder if I could fly.

For seconds, very long seconds, I knew that it was possible.
I knew it.

Then like the shock of a plunge pool, the chill damp of waking would strike my senses. The certainty slipped away like dew in the rising summer sun.

I could not.
At least, not yet.

I was young, just a child, when I started to dream that I could fly.

These dreams were so vivid that I had to convince myself, speaking out loud, that this wasn't practical or possible. But I was sure that with enough practice what happened in my dreams would, one day, manifest itself in reality.

In those dreams I knew just how hard and fast to run before I lifted off from the ground. I didn't need to flap my arms. That was far too crude. Arms only came into play to hold my balance, and Soar like an eagle. Obviously.

Since I was living in a convent children's home from the age of seven to fourteen, not surprisingly my flight looked down upon the fields and trees that were the 70 acres of our childhood playground.

As I grew older I became more confident and skilled in my dreams. The fear I had of flying much higher than the huge oak and the horse chestnut trees eventually gave way to laughter and screams of delight.

In fact, even into my 20s, those dreams included teaching other children and teenagers how easy it was to lift off from the ground with minimal runway space. Decades later I can still feel the pounding of my heart as I soared above those Hertfordshire fields and meadows divided by hawthorn bushes and gravel paths.

It wasn't until many years later that my dreams were thrust before me in the shape of a story, a fable, which captured the imagination of the world.

It was the story of *Jonathan Livingston Seagull*.

This beautiful, mesmerising little book, written by Richard Bach, tells of a seagull bored with the daily squabbles over food; bored with the daily round of grabbing and gorging, of getting and begetting.

He is seized by a passion for flight – flight for its own glorious sake. Eventually outcast because of his passion and unwillingness to conform, he is taken by two gulls to a higher plane of existence. There, he meets the wisest gull, Chiang.

Chiang teaches Jonathan how to move to anywhere in the universe, instantly. Then he sends Jonathan back to earth to find others like him and bring them his learning and to spread his love for flight.

I've been haunted for years by the parallels this fable has with the creation of extraordinary businesses.

Businesses whose **Purpose** goes beyond conquering and consuming; beyond **Power** and acquisition.

Businesses which model how to create something magical, which take themselves, and others, to a level where everybody is changed – financially, intellectually, emotionally and spiritually transformed.

I wondered, those many years ago, how this could be done.

Now I know.

My suspicion is that *you* want to be part of taking your business, your life – maybe even your industry and your profession – into a better future.

My suspicion is that you're also one of those outlandish souls, the heretics among us, who want to carve their own path, rather than slavishly follow someone else's.

The ones who look, and say, *"By 'eck! I think the majority have got this completely wrong! There's a much, much better way of doing this."*

Isn't that why you're here – reading this?

This book, this journey of flight we're about to take, is for you.

So, are you ready?

Ready to be a heretic?

Ready to lead a richer life, in the fullest sense of the word?

Ready to uncover answers, where others don't yet understand the questions?

Ready to live life on your terms, while creating something extraordinary?

Ready to make a greater difference in people's lives, whilst feeling more fulfilled and excited about your work?

Ready to Soar to places untravelled, which lead, in the words of Minnie Louise Haskins, *"towards the hills and the breaking of day"*?

But a word of warning before you dive in.
This book is a parable; it has different levels of meaning.

The question is... how deep will you go?
Will you find the underlying message, before the end of this Journey?

Look for it. It's there. It's in the whisper of the wind. It's under your wings. It's in the landscape patterns beneath you. It's woven between the lines. Look for it, until you find it.

As I think about that little child, gliding and whooshing and sweeping through the skies, I always wondered how I could bring others with me.

This, this book, this Journey, is the start.

Come... Soar with me.

Chapter 1

You're About to See What Transformation Looks Like

This isn't about more business **information**.

This isn't even about more **inspirational ideas**.

The journey to greater impact – to doing great work – requires **transformational** thinking and behaviour.

Of course, this assumes that you want to create something that is truly meaningful, and a legacy that lasts.

It Started Here

I first spotted Mary in Guildford, Surrey.
Tall, slim, simply yet elegantly dressed, bespectacled, and with auburn hair. She sat in the audience, concentrating hard and taking notes, as I presented a three-hour workshop.

My first phone conversation with her was fascinating.

Mary didn't start business life as a financial planner (I mean, who does?). She had been a chartered accountant since leaving university. She'd moved from Deloitte to eventually take on various financial director roles.

But that didn't satisfy her yearning to be in control of her business destiny. She'd had enough of being an employee. She wanted to experience more adventure, more meaning and **Purpose**, in her work. She longed for a sense of contribution beyond figures and percentages.

So, here she was, in her mid-50s, having changed her successful career to become a fully qualified Chartered Financial Planner. Some might have said she was barmy!

She described her life to me working and studying *"a million hours a week"* as a financial planner attached to a high-profile firm just south of London.

As we spoke, I felt for her, trapped as she was on a hamster wheel of busy-busy activity. If she had enjoyed a break at weekends, that would have been something. But it didn't happen too often.

Recognise This Story?

Worse than the exhaustion was her feeling of rejection and failure. Meeting after meeting ended with potential clients going away to "think about it".
It's not surprising that this knocked her confidence.

Her low self-esteem presented itself in her inability to charge a decent level of fee, given her skill, knowledge and hard-won life experience.

A fee of £1,500 per annum was about all she could muster. In her expensive – and wealthy – area of the country, it wasn't a good reflection of her skills.

What I heard in that first conversation was irritation, exhaustion, disappointment.

Why The Frustration?

Well, put yourself in her shoes.

Firstly, you can't sell to save your life. (*But*, you ask yourself, *does financial planning have to be about selling? Surely not!*)

Instead, you realise what you *do* have is a way of helping people relax – and feel in control – in your presence.

You've a solid financial background, with years of seeing how businesses work well (or not).

You've studied hard and are technically proficient. You're organised, determined, and know you have something to offer.

But more than that. Much more. You care.

You care about your clients. You care about people's hardships. You hate to see people confused, in chaos, fearful or suffering. And you have the natural empathy and insight into people's feelings, that men consciously try to learn, and women tend to possess more naturally.

What She Wanted

As we spoke for a second and then third time, it became clear to me what Mary didn't want. She wasn't interested in acquiring things... more possessions or grander property. She wasn't chasing power or popularity.

Mary revealed what she wanted most of all...

→ *"Wouldn't it be a delicious luxury to throttle down to a four-day working week, long before I retire?"*

→ *And what would be even better,"* she went on, *"would be to spend more time out of the office, walking the hills and cliffs of Dorset – in fact, all around Britain's coastline – with my husband and our dogs."*

Yet, sitting there, talking to me, she didn't see how any of this was practical.

And you've probably felt the same yearnings in your business life.

Something Different

On the face of it, Mary didn't meet my criteria for new coaching clients. She wasn't even close:

→ She was too new to financial planning.
→ She wasn't creating nearly enough revenue to show me that she had mastered her craft.
→ She wasn't the leader of her firm, so, in principle, couldn't make the independent decisions I'd be asking of her.

But... but...

I sensed something distinctly different about her. Something that drove her to continue striving for an answer. Mary had a **Purpose** beyond making a living. A **Purpose** etched deep in the memory of her childhood.

The Clue Was in Her Tears

She still carried the memory of watching her unhappy mother resigned to her fate in a miserable marriage. Trapped financially.

As Mary spoke about it, tears welled up, and her chin quivered, quite unlike the controlled, confident individual of just moments before.

By the time she had started carving out her career, her pain had evolved into a determination to do two things:

→ **Firstly**, she would learn how to use money wisely to provide financial independence and freedom. She would never allow herself to be so trapped.
→ **Secondly**, one day she would find a way to help other women who find themselves confused, fearful and trapped by their lack of financial knowledge.

Mary was driven by a **Purpose**.

And it was that **Purpose** that deeply impressed me.

"Help me," she said. *"Help me to become the person, the professional, the business, that women on the verge of painful divorce turn to."*

And so I did.

We Started The Journey

We embarked together on a well-tested, step-by-step Journey:

→   There were searching coaching conversations.
→   There were group masterclasses and teleconferences.
→   There was email coaching, copywriting, role-playing.
→   She needed guidance in designing new services and client material.

The journey was emotional, illuminating and satisfying to be part of. Mary was like a dog at a bone, relentlessly implementing what she had learned.

What was most surprising was Mary's attitude. She seldom argued. She left her ego at the door. Once she understood a principle or practice, she acted. Whatever I recommended, she did it. Immediately.

Rare. Particularly in any male-dominated business sector, where egos abound.

The Delightful Science

As you read, you might be forgiven for thinking that Mary's journey relied solely on her **Passion** and sense of **Purpose**. They were important, yes. But there was more to her decisions than that.

Underlying her journey, Mary discovered science and substance, principles and practices based on **carefully-researched empirical evidence**. They were learnable, logical and independent of charisma or sales skills.

Mary was delighted. She could stop **persuading** and focus on **serving**.

> Mary discovered... principles and practices based on carefully-researched, empirical evidence. They were learnable, logical and independent of charisma or sales skills.

Now Look at Her!

As one of our VIP guests, Mary attended our Soul Millionaire Summer MasterClass in 2017.

I'd invited her to be one of three clients/guests who would give a progress report on their Journeys.

As I watched her enter the room, she radiated confidence, and glowed with a quiet satisfaction as she spoke.

She told us of the two prestigious business awards she'd won in the previous six months, with a third expected.

She explained that clients continue to line up to see her.

Meanwhile, solicitors invite her to their offices, and introduce her to their new client, saying: *"Allow me to introduce you to your financial planner, Mary."*

Before meeting her, new clients already know that her minimum annual fee is six times what she charged mere months ago.

More importantly, she understands how (and why) to charge fees separately to financial products. These are real fees, not commissions by another name.

Truth be told, she has broken the mould for her profession.

That's Not The Question

Now, you might be thinking: *Well, I don't deal with such wealthy or high-net-worth clients, so how is this relevant to me?*

If that thought has crossed your mind, then perhaps you're asking the wrong question. But don't worry. We have time. And you will be crystal clear about the real question, by the time you've finished reading this book.

I'd recommend a different kind of question, perhaps two:

→   What do others see in Mary and her business that warrants high recognition of her work?

→   And how has she redesigned her professional role so that clients are attracted to her, and ready to pay multiples of what they would pay to other financial advisers and planners?

Decide to Be Different, Not Just Better

Firstly, it's important to understand this: she doesn't receive those fees because she seeks out wealthier clients.

She's paid six times what she used to be paid, because she has learned how to make her service different, more client-relevant, more valued.

But It's More Than That

If I let you leave this story thinking, *Ah! This kind of financial success is the point of Mary's efforts!* then you'd be missing the point.

You see, Mary's interpersonal skills have an unusual impact on the wellbeing of every client who engages with her. Her work (and the way she works):

→ Reduces her clients' fears.
→ Renews their hope.
→ Replenishes their peace of mind.
→ Revitalises their relationships at home.
→ Regenerates their aspirations for a better future.

I urge you to pause here, to ponder this list.
Because these are natural outcomes of a service founded upon *The Flight of The Soul Millionaire.*

This is not about tidying up clients' finances, saving them tax, or improving the performance of some investments. The impact we're looking at is emotional, mental, physical – even spiritual.

Listen to Her Explanation

Many business leaders tell me, *"We'd like to make a real difference."* I'm sure they're earnest in their desire. If that's the case, this story is just one example of what "difference" truly looks like.

Life by life, Mary is transforming the world around her. And, in the eyes and words of her clients, *"Working with Mary is like nothing we've ever experienced in business before"*. It's life-changing.

This is the way she explains it:

"I believe that I have the best job in the world!

Underlying all that I do is a Purpose about which I'm Passionate: to help women who are in a stressful and vulnerable situation.

Add to that the coaching and questioning skills I've learned, helping me to change the lives of these clients, not merely reorganise their money.

What's more, the carefully-structured Journey I've travelled has given me the confidence to charge an unusual level of fees.

What's behind my work? Well, because I believe that money, on its own, has little value, I'm satisfied that the work I do is far less about my clients' money and far more about each client's life!"

The Question Is: Are You Asking The Right Questions?

Right now, you probably have a few, don't you?
I'd be surprised if you didn't.

Questions like:

→　How did Mary learn to think and behave so differently from other financial advisers and planners? And in a way that few business leaders would ever dare?

→　Why do clients flock to her, already aware of what she charges? Why do they ignore other skilled financial planners within their radius?

→　Why do solicitors regularly organise formal introductions to Mary, confidently instructing their clients to work with her?

→　Why has she rejected much of the assumed wisdom that is being spread around the so-called 'best-practice' circuit?

→　What allowed her to see that the comfortable traditions that abound in the financial services sector are unhelpful, and paralyse the will to change?

→　Finally, what exactly is this Journey she undertook, to more than fulfil her dreams within a few months?

Heart of Gold, Mind of Steel

The answers to the questions I've posed are what drove me to give birth to this book.

You see Mary recognised that **Passion** and **Purpose** alone would not create the results that she wanted. Certainly, she quickly understood that they are the Heart of Gold of a business. They can be catalysts, emotional drivers, which lift an organisation to greater performance.

She also appreciated that even gritty effort wouldn't do. She already worked her socks off each week.

No, her decades of business experience told her that commercial discipline, a Mind of Steel, was part of the equation.

What she sought was a coherent strategy, a framework, which would add science to the art.

The Journey she spoke about is just such a strategy, a framework, a disciplined approach to her professional role of Adviser.

The Journey brings together that Heart of Gold and Mind of Steel.

Where those behaviours overlap is the sweet spot of superior business accomplishment.

Mary put that sweet spot to great use.

So, come with me now on that Journey.

Let me show you what has been right under your nose since you were a child.

Let me show you what has been staring at us since the dawn of mankind.

Let me show you what everybody has enjoyed, yet nobody in the UK has ever thought to apply to business accomplishment.

Let me show you those who have gone beyond Success... to Significance... by following this Journey.

Come. Fly with me to new heights.

The Thinking Bench

In 2004, when I first started coaching full time, my children bought a lovely Father's Day present. It was a bench.

They noticed that I loved to sit, think and ponder in my garden if I was wrestling with a personal or business idea or problem.

They called it *The Thinking Bench*. And so it became.

It sat in the shade of a beautiful magnolia tree. As a concept, it found its way into my first book, *The Soul Millionaire*.

From The Thinking Bench flowed five years of fortnightly blogs and e-zines. Creative ideas galore helped me to make sense of my life, launching a totally new career, with unfamiliar rules for success.

But, sadly, I stopped producing it, as my business became more successful and more demanding.

Now, in writing this book, my wife, Wendy, as well as one of my coaches, Andrew, followed by my editor, Jo... have combined forces to persuade me, crying, *"David, it's time to bring back The Thinking Bench!"*

It's time that I listened.

At the end of each chapter, I'll invite you to sit with me on The Thinking Bench. I'll share some concluding thoughts and personal musings with you.

After that, I'll invite you to consider the chapter you've just read. I'll encourage you to engage with the questions that have arisen in those pages, and within yourself. Doing this, you'll make this Journey an **experience**, rather than just a casual read.

What Have You Learned?

→　What do you see as the driving factors behind the transformation in Mary's circumstances?

→　What frustrations do you face in common with Mary?

→　What are your thoughts on why clients now pay her six times more than before?

→　What traditions do you see in your business sector that are hindering your progress?

→　What examples have you seen in your industry where a successful business might not be technically better, but is certainly different?

What Will You Do Now?

→　Can you list three practices or principles from this chapter that, when applied, could improve the results in your business?

→　Which one would you act on first?

→　What skill would you most like to learn that you believe Mary has developed on the journey she has taken?

Chapter 2

You Have
a Story.
And You're
The Hero

Now you discover the ageless model, which underpins almost every story of ordinary folk who embark upon extraordinary journeys...

And you come to see why such a life-changing story could be **Your** story...

And that **You** can be the Hero.

Listen to The Awakening of a Hero

"Would you like some bread, Sir?"
A simple enough question. But the answer nearly cost Matthew his life. And transformed that life. Forever.

It was Matt and Katherine's Las Vegas honeymoon. They'd upgraded to their hotel's penthouse suite. Life was very good.

But that innocent piece of bread would spell the end of their honeymoon. It plunged Matt into a three-week fight for survival. You see, he is allergic to nuts. The bread had become contaminated.

From somewhere in the fog of life-threatening anaphylactic pain he heard a medic ask an insane question: *"Are you sure you want to be treated?"*

(Of course, the real question was: *"Can you afford the $1,100 for this ambulance?"*)

Katherine had to beg and plead with doctors and nurses for an hour, as Matt writhed on the bed. Eventually, doctors took the trouble to discover that their medication had created deadly pancreatitis.

Three weeks later, Matt was out of hospital. They were back home. Sobered. Wiser. Over long hours, they reflected upon their experience. And on medical bills of £210,000.

Even if they'd sold their home and the shirt off Matt's back, they would still have been bankrupt. All hail good travel insurance (particularly when it pays out, as Matt's did!).

Take Note of His Transformation

I doubt whether it's possible to go through such an experience without changing perspective. The Critical Few matters of life tend to stand out more clearly from The Trivial Many.

Matt is certainly a changed man.

Meeting him is like engaging with a 49-year-old in a 29-year-old body.

He is painfully aware that Life has given him a second chance.

He has trodden a path, a Journey, that few at his age have experienced.

He sees, with crystal clarity, how easy it is to be consumed in the pursuit of things that, ultimately, don't matter.

Chasing, and grasping for, possessions, property, popularity, prestige and the illusion of power. None of this matters to him any longer.

How he can create deeper relationships to serve those around him is now Matt's overriding concern.

Matt's work changes lives. To me, he is a Hero on an exciting Journey.

(What's interesting is that his two businesses have taken off like a rocket! Revenue has grown tenfold. Behind that growth is a team just as passionate as he is about its work and the impact its members have on clients.)

Heroes Are Made, Not Born

Babies don't arrive as ready-made Heroes.

The Heroes they become are formed and shaped. Often by hard, heart-wrenching experiences.

But we don't have to look far to see the impact that such Heroes have on the world around them. Each of us can name our favourites: men and women whose character-stretching Journey has given them the **Power** to reshape their world.

There are some life Journeys that do that:

→   To you.
→   To your business.
→   To those who support you.
→   To those you serve.

This Chapter starts to explain the *why, what* and *how* of such transformative Journeys.

Are You Sitting Comfortably?

Whatever your age... whatever your taste... whatever your philosophy, culture or religion, one thing that weaves us together is the power of **Story-telling**.

This pattern of communication is how **Principles** and **Truths** have been passed down from parent to child, from teacher to student, from mentor to apprentice.

It would seem that **Story-telling** has been at the heart of how we share the essence of our thoughts and beliefs – probably from the dawn of mankind.

So, let's look at some of these stories. You'll easily recognise them. It's likely that they and their characters have influenced billions of lives over the centuries:

The Lord of the Rings. Harry Potter. Star Wars. **Moses, Prince of Egypt.** *The Hunger Games. The Last Samurai. Avatar.* **Jesus Christ.** *Jane Eyre. The Pilgrim's Progress. Great Expectations. Beauty and the Beast. The Lion King. Aladdin. The Greatest Showman. Titanic. Cinderella. Hacksaw Ridge. Spider-Man...*

These parables, these allegories, fairy stories, legends – they're powerful. They pierce through our intellect. They cut right through to our very souls. They are indelibly emblazoned into our memories, typically from childhood.

Look Again. Right Under Your Nose

Did you spot it?

Did you spot the thread running through every story I mentioned above?

It took me decades, and a little book called *The Dream Giver* by Bruce Wilkinson, to recognise that **there is a common pattern to much of the Story-telling we know and love.**

The evidence suggests that this common pattern has been present since the emergence of **Story-telling** itself.

As Disney would sing, from *Beauty and the Beast*, it's a *"tale as old as time"*.

The story titles I mentioned weren't selected at random. The fact is, they all follow a pattern, an astonishing structure. And that's what makes each of them so spell-binding, so moving and so memorable.

So, what is this astonishing structure?

Why does it appear so consistently and recognisably in drama, religious writings and ritual, music, dance and myths?

More importantly... why, oh why, does it matter to your business?

Well, I'll tell you.
The pattern is called *The Hero's Journey*.

It's a pattern first recognised and articulated by 20th-century American author Joseph Campbell, in his book of the same name.

I've shown a very brief, graphical summary of The Hero's Journey in Figure 1 (p.35).

"In a sense, life is about our forceful – often overpowering – need to take journeys.

The problem is... our tendency is to grip our 'swings in the playground' tightly, even though – if we'd just let go – there's an amazing 'trampoline' just around the corner, which we'd love so much better."

Adapted from Robert E Quinn

Do Something That Matters

The reason that The Hero's Journey is so powerful is because it's all about transformation.

Transformation of the individual – The Very Ordinary Hero – as they go out to achieve great deeds on behalf of the group, the community or the civilisation.

Transformation of their skills, their courage, their strengths, their character.

Transformation – because of their heroic Journey – of the lives of the people around them.

Isn't that what heroes do?
Isn't that why they strike a chord with every generation?

Wouldn't you and I like to be just such a Hero... if only for a small moment?

Just once in our lives, wouldn't each of us like to do something that is deeply meaningful, memorable, lastingly influential and transformative?

The fact that all these questions are largely rhetorical is why discovering The Hero's Journey was such a pivotal moment in my business life.

In one of those flashes of breathless *I-can't-believe-what-I'm-seeing!* moments, I recognised that The Hero's Journey was not merely interesting; it could be a foundational path in taking businesses to that elusive Next Level.

"Supposing," as we used to say as children. *"Just supposing... a business, a leader, a team could be so transformed. What then?"*

What if The Hero's Journey could become the foundation for any business? *Your* business?

Take My Hand, Journey With Me

So, come with me step-by-step through the structure of The Hero's Journey.

See for yourself why it's so enduring, illuminating... and understandable.

> Just once in our lives, wouldn't each of us like to do something that is deeply meaningful, memorable, lastingly influential and transformative?

Once you see it for yourself, I believe you'll begin to understand what I saw.

You'll begin to see why the businesses that have walked (even part of) the Journey have emerged with their own stories of life-changing outcomes, for them, their clients and their communities.

To make the Journey easy to visualise, I'd like you to imagine just one of the stories, films or characters mentioned above – just one.

Hold that story and character firmly in your mind at each step of the Journey.

For example, you might choose:

→ Katniss Everdeen of *The Hunger Games.*
→ Perhaps Frodo in *The Lord of the Rings.*
→ Or Jake Sully from *Avatar.*
→ Maybe Aladdin, since you might have seen the Disney film (or joined me in watching the Disney musical, with my daughter in the cast!).

Picture your Hero and hold their image at the front of your mind, throughout this chapter.

Write down the name of your Hero... right here:

_____

_____

Now let's follow your Hero on their Journey.
Take them with you throughout every paragraph in this chapter.

You'll see how the pattern holds true, whatever the story you've chosen.

Start where you are.

The Eight Stages of The Hero's Journey

There are eight simple stages to this Hero's Journey and the new world beyond.

Stage 1: The awakening, the call, the refusal

In this first stage, our Hero is minding their own business in a comfortable world.

But there's something not right. Something irritating.
Maybe they're bored. Restless.

Suddenly, a force rocks their comfortable life. It's like a sound slap across the back of the head. It's either an external force or event. Or something rises from deep within them. It's a Call – a Call to change.

At first, our Hero refuses to heed the Call, fearing the unknown. In some stories, people in the Hero's life – particularly those close to them – also try to dissuade the Hero from changing the status quo. The friends, family or community are unsettled. *"If it works, don't fix it!"* they cry.

Stage 2: The teacher appears

Perhaps someone appears in the Hero's life – a wise, experienced traveller of foreign worlds – who gives the Hero advice, training, equipment... whatever is needed.

At other times the Teacher is a newly discovered source of insight, courage or wisdom bubbling up from deep inside the Hero.

Either way, the Teacher ensures that the Hero learns a new set of truths. These truths help him to see things, and the future, as he could never have imagined before.

Do Something You've Never Done

Stage 3: The Mission preparation

Our Hero starts to appreciate the size and nature of his awesome Mission. At times he is overwhelmed with doubt.

But the Teacher, and others, rally to support him. They encourage him through difficult **Preparation** and learning, before he is ready to cross the threshold into a new, unknown world.

Stage 4: The Mission is accepted. The Hero steps into the new world

It's now that the Hero *gets it*, as my children would say.
Not only does he *get it*. But he commits to leaving his comfortable world and entering a world that feels frightening.

This reminds me of that wonderful poem by Minnie Louise Haskins, quoted in King George VI's Christmas Message in the dark days of 1939:

And I said to the man who stood at the gate of the year:
"Give me a light that I may tread safely into the unknown."

And he replied:
"Go out into the darkness and put your hand into the Hand of God.
That shall be to you better than light and safer than a known way."

So, I went forth, and finding the Hand of God, trod gladly into the night.
And He led me towards the hills and the breaking of day in the lone East.

Keep Your Friends Close, Keep Your Enemies Closer

Stage 5: The opposition and friendships

Almost from his first steps into The New World, the Hero meets intense opposition.

What balances this are the allegiances that arise. They tend to arise when our Hero makes it clear that he's committed to change. It's this Courageous Clarity that is the 'tipping point' that magnetises new, supportive relationships.

These new allies join the Teacher in helping our Hero to better understand the Mission. Meanwhile, they surround him in battling against foes – seen or unseen – who would have paralysed his intentions with fear.

Stage 6: The Wilderness Test

'Wilderness' is the term I use for "The Unknown World".

This is the alien world into which the Hero must step or stay forever frozen by yesterday's habits.

Every hero – even accompanied by allies – must endure this period of Wilderness Testing. Otherwise, an adventure can hardly be called an *adventure,* can it?

No oasis appears to ease their weariness. The daunting trek feels relentless. And our band of heroes are constantly hampered and harried by attacks along the way. Faith and courage are their greatest weapons now.

It would be much easier to give up.
Not doing so is what begins the development of a Hero!

"And I said to the man who stood at the gate of the year: 'Give me a light that I may tread safely into the unknown.'

And he replied:
'Go out into the darkness and put your hand into the Hand of God.

YOU HAVE A STORY. AND YOU'RE THE HERO

That shall be to you better than light and safer than a known way."'

Minnie Louise Haskins

You Sure You're Ready For This...?

Stage 7: The final test; the road home

In the midst of the Wilderness Test, our Hero faces Death. If it's not Death, then it's the Hero's greatest fear, come to haunt him.

From this pivotal moment comes the transformation of our Hero.

In some stories our Hero must actually die, before being brought forth to life as a wiser, more powerful, awe-inspiring being. Someone who commands respect, even reverence, as a result of this test.

Often, as a result of this Final Test, our Hero returns with a treasure – perhaps a sword, an elixir, or some other symbol of power.

Our Hero then heads home, sometimes losing allies on the way.

Stage 8: The new Mission

Our Hero arrives at the place he longed for. Perhaps it's the home that he left, and which he has saved from dark forces.

But something has changed. Typically, it's neither the place, nor its people. It's the Hero. He can no longer go back to being who he was.

Although he energetically works to improve the world he's returned to/ arrived at, our Hero is restless once more. Something feels unfinished.

Then, one day, he spots a young person heading his way, clearly wishing to speak with him.

"I've had the weirdest feeling for some time," says our young person.

"It's a feeling that something is about to happen. In fact, it's more than a feeling. I've had this recurring dream. And it's terrifyingly real!

It's about me going on an adventure. You know, a slaying-the-bad-giants-and-dragons sort of adventure. I start travelling to a place, just over the horizon, where somebody keeps calling my name. Frightening things start happening. I can hardly face night time.

Can I talk to you about it?"

Now our Hero knows what he has been prepared for.
Now **he** has become the Teacher!

"So, tell me," our Hero asks, *"what does this adventure look like?"*

"It's crazy. You'll never believe me when I tell you," says the young person.

"Try me!" responds our Hero, smiling.

Figure 1: The Hero's Journey
A simple summary of the Eight Stages of The Hero's Journey

1	**The Awakening, Call & Refusal**	Shaken from Comfort
2	**The Teacher Appears**	Taught the Truth

3	**The Mission Preparation**	Training for The Unknown World
4	**Crosses Threshold to New World**	Owns the Mission, Steps Into The Unknown World

5	**The Friendships & Opposition**	Builds Allies, Faces Foes & Tests
6	**The Wilderness Test**	Battles, Learns to Lead, Endures

7	**Final Test, Reward, Travel Home**	Faces Death, Returns With Prize
8	**The New Mission**	Ignites Others to See Their Mission

Go On, Ask The Question!

Are you asking the question yet?
You know. The Question.

Because, if you're not, then I've probably lost you altogether.

It's that old *Field of Dreams* kind of question: *"What's [this] got to do with baseball?"*

The question has to be:

"That's all very interesting. But... what's this got to do with me and my business?"

I'm glad you asked.
Because that's where we're going next.

The Thinking Bench

Our eldest daughter had gained her degree. But wasn't sure in which direction she was pointing in life.

Until she went to Africa.

Mum, trustee of a children's charity, had organised another 10-day expedition. And Lauren fancied another adventure: building school extensions, creating water towers, installing computers, and a safari to round off the trip.

Except she wasn't ready for the children.

The children who constantly, constantly smiled... whilst dancing in a playground of questionable puddles.

The children who were excited that they would get more than one bowl of *fufu* that day.
The children who sang to her. Haunting, harmonising songs.
The children who stroked her silky hair, and golden arms.
The children who laughed and screamed with delight at her shimmying to the music.

Eventually, her heart broke.
And she disappeared for hours, to sit quietly. Staring.
Lauren woke up to the person she could become.

First, she completed a Master's degree.

Then, whilst her friends entered high-paying, glamorous-sounding careers in and around London... Lauren chose to enter the charity sector.

Since then, she has travelled across the world... ultimately bringing hope, saving lives.

There are moments in our business lives when Destiny tries to get our attention.
Sometimes it's a constant tap on the shoulder.
Sometimes it's a good thwack across the back of the head.
The message? *"Wake up!"*

I wonder.

Is there a *"Wake up!"* message you might be ignoring today?

What Have You Learned?

→   Can you pinpoint a moment in life – particularly in business – that shook you up and made you change for the better?

→   What *call to change* could you be ignoring right now – because it frightens you?

→   Who is the next Teacher in your life? Who could show you the way, and help you turn your Good work to Great work?

→   Are you walking where the herd grazes, fat and content? Or have you stepped onto 'The Road Less Traveled', where the future starts?

→   Are you complaining about the Wilderness you're trekking through? Or do you see that there's a reason for you being tested: something that life wants you to learn?

What Will You Do Now?

→   What need-to-improve is staring you in the face today, which you're going to have to face up to in 12 months?

→   What's the one step you could take to test out your crazy but magnificent idea?

→   What conversation do you need to have today... that might create the ally you need to lift you to higher accomplishment?

Chapter 3

The Soul Millionaire Journey is Born

What emerges is a framework
that creates empowered people.

What's more surprising is that
the same framework improves
how leaders behave, how teams
excel and how revenue increases.

This is how businesses are elevated
to levels they previously spoke about
only in moments of wishful thinking.

Beware The Ascot Headbutt

It's a favourite of mine: scrambled eggs and smoked salmon (on brown toast).
In some parts of the world it's called Eggs Ascot.

I walked into the Moran Hotel, looking for my host.
She wasn't difficult to spot; she has one of the most memorable smiles on the financial services circuit.

We settled down, with eggs on order.

"Well, you called the meeting," she started. *"What's on your mind?"*
My cue. I waxed lyrical about the possibilities and opportunities of working more closely together.

I stopped for breath as my Eggs Ascot arrived.

She smiled at me. That smile. And responded...
"Dave, that all sounds great. Really it does..."

I held my breath. I could distinctly hear a *"But..."*
I was right.

"But... I don't think I want to work any closer with you."

"What!" I blurted out.
"Then what on earth am I doing up here in Chiswick at this ridiculous hour?!"

"It's a good question," she calmly continued.
"So, let me explain why I'm saying what I'm saying."
With a mouthful of toast and smoked salmon, what else could
I do but listen?

**"The problem with you, Mr Scarlett, is that you've lost track of who
you are.** *You've become really boring, just like the rest of the consultants
dropping into this market."*

And then the neat headbutt followed.

*"You've gone all marketing-schmarketing in the last few years.
And you sound no different to anyone else.
I'll say it again: reeeaaally boring."*

With a delicate coup de grace to follow:

"Whatever happened to The Soul Millionaire, *eh? You know, the
spiritual, quirky, interesting guy that people were talking about?"*

Finally, the ultimatum.

"When I see you going back to being **that** *guy,* **then** *I'll be happy to talk
to you. In the meantime, I need to get to another meeting quickly.
So, I'll just sip this coffee, pay the bill, and leave you to finish your
scrambled eggs."*

And she was gone.

I wouldn't mind if that was the only experience during that year telling me truths I'd rather not hear.

Within weeks, I'd met marketing consultant Carrie, who said, *"Well, I've read your* Soul Millionaire *book. But I can't for the life of me see what that has to do with your current brand and activity, The Adviser Gym."*

Not long afterwards, my mentor, Andrew, said: *"Look, I just don't see how I can help you further with your current business model, teaching marketing strategies to financial advisers. When are you going to exercise the courage to be who you really are:* **The Soul Millionaire**? *That concept you wrote about is unique in the industry you're trying to work with. It's meaningful."*

I'm slow. But even I start to wake from slumber when three people give me the same message from three different perspectives. And all in the same month.

I'll show you how I finally stopped copying others' best practices and started becoming what decades in business had prepared me for.

If Moses Had Received an 11th Commandment, it Might Have Been This:
"Thou Shalt Have a Revelation at The Most Unexpected of Times"

There I was, a-musing and a-pondering about this Hero thing I'd been studying.

Sleep evaded me, because I'd made the mistake of going to bed with a question on my mind.

The question sounded like this: *What exactly is the relationship between the Eight Stages of The Hero's Journey... and running an effective and exciting business?*

It came eventually: that restless sleep.

And when I awoke, I did so with a jolt. My heart palpitating wildly.

I felt like a man possessed. I rushed downstairs, grabbing a pen and notepad from my briefcase. Then started to scribble, demonically. I could scarcely breathe.

I have no idea how long I sat there, arrows and pictures and mind-maps flying from my fingers. But I could see something forming from the manic mess. There on my notepad. Not just something – three somethings.

→ **On the left side** of the page were the Eight Stages of The Hero's Journey.

→ **On the right side** was a summary of results that my coaching clients (mainly financial advisers and planners) had achieved during my previous 10 years of coaching.

→ **Slap in the middle** was the title of my novel, written just seven years previously: *The Soul Millionaire*. (It hadn't fared badly; it had reached Top 20 on Amazon UK for a sliver of time.)

Somehow, in my babbling, excited brain, I knew that my novel held the clue to translating the Hero's Journey theory (left-hand column) into superb business practice (right-hand column).

Don't ask me how. I just knew it!

I had stumbled across the Four Stages of almost any successful adventure.

Not just as they applied to myths and legends, parables and fairy stories. But as they applied to life.

And to business!

Come in Close, Then I'll Know You Can't See

That's what a magician does, isn't it? Gets us to stare so hard at something that we completely miss the something else that's happening before our very eyes.

Often, our vision is most clear when we step away – not when we peer closely.

(We get so busy on our business trek through each day and week focused on where to put our foot next without tripping or falling down a pothole. Or focused on how to survive until the next weekend break, aching for refreshment and blessed rest.)

I think we all recognise that paradox (stepping away to see more clearly) as *gaining perspective.*

It's the perspective we gain atop a mountain or gazing from a clifftop at the might of the sea. Haven't we all experienced that emotional intake of breath, as we view our world with unusual clarity?

Perhaps seeing our life as we've never seen it before?

And that is how I came to understand the business relevance of The Hero's Journey. I had to step away. I had to allow the confetti to settle. I had to allow the pattern to emerge.

And it did. A day or so later.

Put These Specs On, Do You See Elegant Simplicity?

Reviewing The Hero's Journey (left-hand column) showed me the art and science of business through a new set of spectacles. Isn't that what scientists call a *paradigm shift?*

Anyway, with that new insight, I analysed every chapter of *The Soul Millionaire* book (middle column). Somewhere, buried in there, I knew I'd find the clue to *why* walking The Hero's Journey would elevate a business to new heights. Not just any clue – a logical, coherent clue.

After a few hours, I sat back with a sigh of satisfaction. My suspicions were confirmed.

Without question, The Hero's Journey was indeed the skeleton and foundation of that book, *The Soul Millionaire.*

There it was: the tale of the awakening, mission, adventures, and ultimate financial (and business) transformation of the book's Hero, Jonathan.

Even the Teacher appeared, as well as the various friends and foes. And, yes, there was the Wilderness and the tough, gritty times for the Hero.

Towards the end of *The Soul Millionaire* saga, Jonathan realised that his next mission was to be the mentor and teacher for the next Jonathan: the next Hero-to-be.

During this process, the Hero's personal life and relationships evolved into something vastly more meaningful and enjoyable. He grew to understand what it meant to serve, rather than to grasp. He also came to understand the real meaning of love, something quite different to the picture portrayed by Hollywood and the media.

Meanwhile, the Hero's business acumen and financial circumstances didn't just develop, they leapt and bounded.

It was all there!

The Soul Millionaire **book demonstrated that every single stage of The Hero's Journey had relevance when building a superb business... and then again, when taking it to the so-called 'next level'.**

Something else came to light, while reviewing my book. I saw that I could simplify the *Eight Stages* of the Hero's Journey to just *Four Stages.* More became less. And, strangely, less was substantially more.

Simplicity always does it for me.
And the simplicity I saw looked like this (see Figure 2, p.51).

The Pudding is Good to Eat

I had my proof.

The Hero's Journey and the development of a better-than-good business went hand in hand.

Drinking that in, right then and there, I enjoyed another of those serendipitous moments.

Sitting at the edge of my desk happened to be a copy of two books: *Good to Great* and *Built to Last* (by Jim Collins and Jerry Porras, concluding years of research amongst leading, global Visionary Companies).

Just looking at those book covers reminded me that, globally, Visionary Companies have woven those four simplified Hero's Journey stages into the fibre of their thinking, planning and actions.

It was also comforting to review the case studies of my recent clients. They had invariably integrated most (if not all) of those four stages during our work together.

Some of their results you've already started to see in the stories I've mentioned. Others will unfold as you read further.

THE SOUL MILLIONAIRE JOURNEY IS BORN

Figure 2

The Four Stages of The Soul Millionaire (Book)

1 The Big Mission, The Awakened Mind, The Ignited Heart
2 The Preparation, Commitment, Starting The Mission
3 The Inspired 'Warrior' & Friends Face Tests
4 The Hero Returns – Transformed, Ready to Ignite, Lift & Teach Others

The Essence of Those Four Stages

1 Mission Understanding, Insight, Emotional **Ignition**
2 **Engage** with The Mission
3 Demonstrate **Inspired**, Courageous Leadership
4 An Increase - **Elevation** - of Capability, Influence & Legacy

The Soul Millionaire book demonstrated that every single stage of The Hero's Journey had relevance when building a superb business.

Good Idea, Now Make it Memorable

With these Four Stages expressed in such simple terms, the truth hit me.

I had stumbled across the Four Stages of almost any successful adventure.
Not just as they applied to myths and legends, parables and fairy stories. But as they applied to life, and to business!

Here was an approach to business that promised more than just increased revenue and profit.

Specifically, such an approach would:

→ Transform the team's thinking, and their understanding of *service.*
→ Make a greater difference in the lives of their clients.
→ Generate a desire for excellence in the team.
→ Create an underlying working environment of joy.

I had connected the dots, from left to right.
And I had revealed:

→ The Eight Stages of The Hero's Journey.
→ The personal and business adventures of Jonathan in *The Soul Millionaire* book.
→ The in-the-trenches results of coaching financial planners and business leaders.

I'd distilled the whole journey to just Four Stages.

You'd think I'd be satisfied with this, wouldn't you? But I wasn't.
I wanted a message, a verbal brand, that would be:

→   Easy for the world to understand, and
→   Easy for the world to remember.

So, I embarked on more months of testing – workshops, seminars,
client feedback – to see if the discovery which excited me was just
an illusion in my head.

**After six months I was ready to further distil the essence of those
Four Stages.**

Here was the rocket fuel for a business which would
behave wholly differently from its peers.

And So, The Soul Millionaire Journey Was Born!

The process of Revelation had started for me in the Bleak Midwinter.
It reached its culmination under the warm skies of an English
summer afternoon.

I sat on my Thinking Bench, surrounded by the soothing sights,
smells and sounds of my bee-and-butterfly garden, and saw what
I had uncovered.

On my lap was a single sheet of paper, representing many months of hard work. Staring at that sheet, I had one of those *"Oh, my word"* moments.

Before me, there were no longer four phrases, capturing the essence of everything I'd learned in those six months.

There were just *four* WORDS.
Four words you'll see at the bottom of Figure 3, as I show you my thought process.

Figure 3

The Four Stages of The Soul Millionaire (Book)

1 The Big Mission, The Awakened Mind, The Ignited Heart
2 The Preparation, Commitment, Starting The Mission
3 The Inspired 'Warrior' & Friends Face Tests
4 The Hero Returns – Transformed, Ready to Ignite, Lift & Teach Others

The Essence of Those Four Stages

1 Mission Understanding, Insight, Emotional **Ignition**
2 **Engage** with The Mission
3 Demonstrate **Inspired**, Courageous Leadership
4 An Increase – **Elevation** – of Capability, Influence & Legacy

The Four-Word Distillation of "The Soul Millionaire Journey"

1 Ignite
2 Engage
3 Inspire
4 Elevate

Now, I had an understandable, and easily remembered, way of articulating The Soul Millionaire Journey:

1. *Ignite!*
2. *Engage!*
3. *Inspire!*
4. *Elevate!*

It was that simple.

1. *Ignite!*
   You'll ignite the spirit and **Power** of your business to create, and serve, eager, fulfilling, quality clients, who pay you what you're really, really worth.
2. *Engage!*
   You'll engage those clients, and professional alliances, in such a rich relationship that they become your most passionate advocates, evangelists and marketing team.
3. *Inspire!*
   You'll learn how to inspire your clients, and your team, and demonstrably make a meaningful difference in their lives.
4. *Elevate!*
   You'll elevate your influence, your leadership, your time freedom, your revenue, your enjoyment, your impact, your unique capabilities, creating a powerful legacy in many lives.

Figure 4: The Birth of The Soul Millionaire Journey
At a Glance

The Hero's Journey	How It Appeared In The Soul Millionaire Book	The Essence Of the Story	The 4 Headlines of The Soul Millionaire Journey
1a) The Awakening, Call & Refusal 1b) The Teacher Appears	Big Mission, Awakened Mind, Ignited Heart	Mission Insight & **Ignition**	**Ignite!**
2a) Mission Preparation 2b) Crosses Threshold to New World	Preparation, Commitment, Start The Mission	**Engage** With The Mission, Allies & Foes	**Engage!**
3a) Friendships & Opposition 3b) The Wilderness Test	Our Inspired Hero & Friends Face Tests	Inspired, **Inspiring**, Courageous Leadership	**Inspire!**
4a) Final Test, Reward, Travel Home 4b) The New Mission	The Hero Returns – Transformed, Ready to Ignite, Lift & Teach Others	**Elevation** of Capability, Influence & Legacy	**Elevate!**

The Thinking Bench

I was gazing and pondering.

I was sitting on my Thinking Bench, a cool drink beside me and hypnotised by the bumble and honey bees eagerly seeking nectar from the last of the purple echinacea. The late summer sun was weakening, casting a more golden light on green leaves, and the smell of the air was already changing.

I was thinking...

I didn't really discover this, did I? The Soul Millionaire Journey, I mean. I *uncovered* it. Because it was there all the time.

I had written a book, *The Soul Millionaire*, but I'd been blind to its underlying business message.

I'd crafted that book and re-read it ad nauseam. Yet here I was, compelled to study it once more, and coming to know it fully for the first time. Silly, really.

However, I'm comforted when I understand the way in which greater souls than me have *uncovered* magnificent work throughout the centuries.

Let's take Michelangelo.

Legends and myths abound regarding Michelangelo's sculpting of the mesmerising 14-foot statue of David.

It is said that his method of work was to create a wax model of his design, then submerge it in water. As he worked, he let the level of water gradually drop. Then, using different chisels, he sculpted what he could see emerging. And so, David emerged from the depths of a huge block of marble.

The Soul Millionaire Journey felt like that. It emerged.

Biographers say that Michelangelo slept sporadically, usually with his clothes and boots on. And he rarely ate.

Hmmm. We all suffer somewhat to be worthy of our craft. But I draw the line at boots in my bed!

What Have You Learned?

→   What do you feel is the connection between the first two stages of The Hero's Journey and your business being given a jolt of pure energy?

→   What exactly is the mission you believe you've been called to fulfil through your business?

→   Have you read that book *The Soul Millionaire*? Did you spot the *Eight Stages* that the hero, Jonathan, went through?

→   Who do you see as your allies in business? And who, or what, do you believe are your foes and forces arrayed against you?

→   What has been your greatest Wilderness test in the last three years? In what way did you demonstrate courageous leadership during this time?

→   What do you see in your life story that shows you're already on The Hero's Journey?

What Will You Do Now?

→   What steps are you going to take to wake your business up – to *Ignite!* it – in the next 90 days?

→   What is it about your business that most inspires you? And is that where you're spending enough time and energy?

→   What skills and/or services can you develop this year to better *Inspire!* your clients to live more fulfilled lives?

STAGE

1

IGNITE!

What You Need to Know About The Ignite! Stage

Every business has a Soul.

What's more, the Soul of the business exudes a *Spirit*, which is felt by all who touch the business.

To understand how we experience this, think of the *Spirit* of the London Olympics in 2012. That's precisely how people referred to it. That spirit was strong, enthralling, memorable, palpable. It was discussed openly and made real.

This business *Spirit* becomes the unseen beating heart, the essence, of your business' very existence. In other words:

→ It's the perfume of the business' history, ethos and culture.
→ It oozes from every pore, shows in the business' behaviour and informs attitude.
→ It weaves itself through every decision and discussion.
→ It influences direction, shapes the perspective and infuses the language.
→ It defines what the business does, when no one is looking.

And, with the right catalyst, the spirit of the business can be ignited.

What the *Ignite!* stage does is to provide those catalysts, thereby taking the Spirit of the business and setting it alight once more. But this time with an energy, a perspective, a clarity that it has never enjoyed before.

Understanding how this 'setting alight' works, requires us to look at two aspects of the business:

1. Your Purpose
2. Your People

First, Let's Focus on Your Purpose

To do this, we'll need to look at two elements of our Soul Millionaire Journey:

→   **The Awakening** (the Call to, and the Teacher for, your new Mission).
→   **The Three Catalysts** (the factors that, when combined, give you propelling **Power** to launch you on your Journey).

We'll cover these elements in the following two chapters. Combined, they will illuminate *Your Purpose.*

Chapter 4

Your Purpose: The Awakening

There comes a time when Life
and Truth whisper in your ear...
or gently tap you on the shoulder,
to awaken you.

They might even give you a sound
thwack across the face, to abruptly
halt your sleepwalking.

Yet, despite this, too often we shake
ourselves off and continue on as if
nothing has happened.

1. The Awakening, Call & Refusal		**Purpose**
	Ignite!	
2. The Teacher Appears		People

3. Mission Preparation		Preparation
	Engage!	
4. Crosses to New World		Pioneering

5. Friendships & Opposition		Possibility
	Inspire!	
6. The Wilderness Test		Power

7. Final Test, Reward, Travel Home		Prosperity
	Elevate!	
8. The New Mission		Posterity

Wake Up, Alfie!

When I first met him, Alfie was a humble senior administrator in a financial planning support team.
He was a cheeky, chirpy, Saturday-night-alright chappie. You know what I mean when I say he lived for the weekend.

Still single and enjoying it, Alfie continued to bathe in the comforts of life, still living with his parents. Friends, girlfriend, music, good food and drink. And a good job in a small, vibrant company to fund it all.

What more could a bloke want?

Then, one day, he announced to his boss that he fancied taking a six-month sabbatical in the USA. Knowing Alfie, I'm not sure any of us were convinced that he'd return.

It was a trip that he and two friends had dreamed about for months. One of those if-I-don't-do-it-before-I-settle-down-then-I-never-will adventures.

So, I was surprised to see him back, after his hectic bucket-list holiday, having tasted the delights of 28 states and 24 cities in just 12 weeks, finishing in Chicago. More than most Americans will ever undertake, I'll wager.

I remember, even now, how I felt when I slid into his nippy black BMW. As usual, he was collecting me from the station and driving me to his firm's offices. He was calmer somehow. His face registered a new-found assurance behind that smile.

There was real emotion in his voice as he described landing in Lima, Peru. His voice changed again, as he recounted what took place when they eventually reached *"that gold and silver mine in Bolivia"*.

Alfie and his buddies had sauntered up to the shift supervisor of the mine and persuaded him to let them join the men going down. Just for a couple of hours, you understand.

It took a mere £3 sterling to buy their way in.

Excitedly donning the mining gear (helmet, bandana and boots) it wasn't long before they found themselves utterly disorientated, lost and trapped in the deep, black belly of the earth.

As the three of them choked on the hot, pungent, gaseous air, Alfie glanced around at a scene that shook him to the core.

Here, in this black hell, men were smiling and greeting them warmly. Especially since our trio had brought a wad of coca leaves and bottles of water for their new friends. Enough coca to stave off hunger, thirst, pain and fatigue for a few precious hours.

Health and safety rules were non-existent down here in this hellhole. There was little health. And even less safety.

That became obvious the first time one of the miners lobbed a stick of dynamite into the tunnel ahead. Alfie's body felt as if his organs had been punched by the blast.

The sweating, grunting men in these pits don't survive long. To continue beyond the age of 45 is a cause for celebration. One such celebrity pointed to his son and grandson, digging side-by-side.

The grime of the mine was etched into the faces and bodies of every heaving shape around them.

The joking between the friends soon stopped. And our intrepid trio glanced at each other from moment to moment.

They tolerated no more than three hours in that brutal world. Crawling around on hands and knees. Their feet cold and soaking.

Let us out. Let us out. Let us out!

Getting back to the surface required every ounce of willpower and patience. The desperate yearning for daylight, sunshine and birdsong rose from their bellies to choke in their throats before they violently sucked at clean air once more.

Alfie would never forget the slow passage of those few hours. The memory of them was chiselled into the soft tablet of his boyish heart.

Within them he aged a full decade.

"Men occasionally stumble over the truth. But most of them pick themselves up and hurry off as if nothing ever happened."

Winston Churchill

Look at The Impact

The cheeky, chirpy, *'whatever'* chappie that was Alfie had disappeared. Forever.

In his place, behind the same eyes, was a man who relished the privilege and luxury of life in England. He was a free man. The choices and foods and comforts of kings were his. He would likely live long and healthy.

He realised he had more than a job. If he made the decision and paid the price, he saw that this could be a richly rewarding career.

Never again would he complain about Monday mornings and getting to work.
Never. Never.

In the coming months, the change showed in his burgeoning career, in his personal relationships, and in every feature of his countenance.

At work, he grasped responsibility and became a role model to other youngsters in the team. Education started to fill his agenda, rather than nights at the pub.

In the business, he found that he had a voice, and he used it. He boldly shared ideas for improvement with colleagues and directors.

He began to challenge the status quo:

→ He challenged the onerous number of clients each adviser was given to work with.
→ He challenged the way work cascaded confusingly from advisers to paraplanners and administrators.
→ He started to spend more time and energy bringing other support staff up to his level of work excellence.
→ He became a useful foil for ideas from his closest colleagues. He encouraged their continued education. This encouragement would later pay enormous dividends, as their confidence increased.

Yes, Alfie's influence grew. Alfie grew until others heard him, and they paid serious attention to him.

Alfie had received his Call to a New Mission in Life.

He had been invited to step into a new world.

An *Awakening* has that kind of impact.

I'm not talking about a new checklist of discrete business tasks to be performed on top of your already-frenetic weekly to-do list.

What I'm talking about is making a magnificent, life-changing Journey your priority. I'm talking about a framework, a carefully woven tapestry, which rejuvenates businesses and elevates lives.

Change Deeply, or Die Slowly

Not all of us will be faced with a South American mine, like Alfie. Not all of us will be called to endure a gasping episode on the floor, choking to death on the mere trace of a nut, like Matt.

These pivotal episodes don't have to be accompanied by fireworks and fanfare. They don't need abundant YouTube 'likes' or a plethora of grinning selfies posted to Facebook.

The tallest, heaviest door of life can swing widely on the smallest hinge.

Many of us recall our own episodes of **awakening** distinctly. Indeed, we can mark the moment when life changed. Or, rather, when we changed. When *we* grabbed the passing opportunity.

Or we didn't. We didn't, because the change frightened us to death.

So, we chose the slow death of our adventurous spirit instead.

I was privileged to be there, to witness Alfie's unquestionable transformation.

In fact, I enjoyed a number of coaching conversations with Alfie along his Journey. I was there on the day he was ready to take the next step in his career, and he wanted me to help him.

You could say, *"When the Student was ready... the Teacher appeared."*

> I think about the lesson I've learned: which is that life's greatest achievements are attained in serving and elevating others.

What Alfie Did Next

First, within days of returning from South America, Alfie sat alone, and asked himself some fearful questions:

→ *The Journey I'm on now gratifies me today. But where will it take me tomorrow? Or in three years?*

→ *What if I changed what I **have** to do... into something that was fascinating and fulfilling and I was **eager** to do?*

→ *What would change if I led, rather than followed? What would happen if I didn't settle for good enough, even if I'm not formally the business owner or leader?*

Next, Alfie made some decisions:

→ He selected a path that would give him greater influence and control – not just greater earnings.

⇨ Initially, this was through education: he paid a price, with his neck on the line, and his hand in his wallet, sacrificing nights in the pub for hard-earned qualifications.

→ He would no longer allow the status quo to squash his intentions. When he felt that something could be changed for the better, he said so. And then invested effort in helping to change it.

→ He would be more aware of his impact on others and seek feedback about that impact. He would swap ego for personal growth.

What Alfie Got

1. Over a period of three years, Alfie did indeed rise to become a Chartered Financial Planner.
2. Added to this, Alfie started developing professional coaching skills to converse at a much deeper level with clients.
3. His courage in speaking out, and seeing others take notice of his ideas, revealed in him leadership qualities he hadn't appreciated before.
4. With this new courage, he and a colleague saw the real possibility of leading their own firm. But this time in a different way, with a different **Purpose**.
5. Given the blessing of their employer, they co-founded a new brand, a new business.

6. Alfie's rapid growing-up process had given him the maturity, insight and confidence to work with business leaders decades older than himself.
7. Where other twenty-somethings might feel intimidated, his coaching skills allowed him to challenge clients' thinking in the most inspiring way.
8. Finally, he was ready to serve multi-millionaire technology entrepreneurs, in a way few other businesses can.

All of that from a couple of hours in a mine in Bolivia!

By reaching this point in your reading, your heart has already started this Soul Millionaire Journey. You just need to bring the rest of you along.

Come With Me to

The Thinking Bench

The two-minute video ended.
So, I looked around the room.

And there were tears.
From men and women.
Unashamed, unabashed tears.

One of those present wrote to me later, to express how comforting
it was being in a room of non-judgmental people.
Which meant that they didn't have to act a part...

They didn't have to be professional (whatever that means)...

They could be authentic.

That happened on a Wednesday.

By Friday I was driving down to Chichester, to meet one of my favourite people in business: Andrew Walsh, my former mentor and dear friend.

Andrew has held various senior roles, from Group Financial Director of a quoted PLC, to Non-Exec Director of three European banks.

He can be tough, logical and driven when needed.
But he's also unusually sensitive, insightful and compassionate.

As we stood outside Chichester Cathedral he told me of the closing remarks made at each of the series of leadership programmes that he delivers.

Having watched strutting, hard-bitten senior executives strip away their posturing and posing, he often observes board members' reactions as those executives share episodes from their life stories.

Every time, tears flow.
Unashamed, unabashed tears.

Then he concludes with something quite ridiculous in British and European business circles. He tells these tough, sometimes ruthless, men...

That he loves them.
Loves them!

By working with them in this vulnerable, unusual way, he helps them to transform their powers of leadership faster than merely informing, persuading and encouraging.

He takes them on an unexpected Journey.

In sharing *Wake Up, Alfie!* with you, I'm advocating a Journey that I've travelled myself. This is not something I dug up from a book or learned on a business course; it's woven into my life and into the lives of those I've travelled with; it's woven into the businesses and lives of those I've coached and mentored – inside and outside of my profession.

If I consider all that I have learned in my Journey, perhaps the most potent is this: **life's greatest accomplishments and joys are attained in serving and lifting others.**

To make a difference (starting with those closest to me); to change the world around me – these are aspirations worth striving for.

This chapter, and those that follow – indeed, this Soul Millionaire Journey – is largely about *how* you can do that, using your business as a conduit.

In our **Awakening,** life calls us to consider new paths: new ways of thinking, behaving and being. And, by 'new ways', I'm not talking about a new checklist of discrete business tasks to be performed on top of your already-frenetic weekly to-do list.

What I'm talking about is making a magnificent, life-changing Journey your priority. I'm talking about a framework, a carefully woven tapestry, which rejuvenates businesses and elevates lives.

What's interesting is this: by reaching this point in your reading, **your heart has already started this Soul Millionaire Journey. You just need to bring the rest of you along.**

What Have You Learned?

→ Which *Wake Up, Alfie!* experience do you feel has had the greatest impact on your life?

→ Did that experience come as a single event, which changed your perspective? Or did it come to you in the form of frustration with your work?

→ What *Wake Up, Alfie!* experience has been driven by roles or relationships in your personal life?

→ How did your *Wake Up, Alfie!* experience grab your attention: as a Still Small Voice in a quiet moment; or as a serious thwack across the head in your normal routine?

→ Looking back, what habit, routine or *settling for* can you now see was enslaving you at the time?

→ Did *The Call* make immediate sense? Or did it seem inconvenient, counter-intuitive and illogical?

→ And did you initially try to ignore or rationalise it away?

What Will You Do Now?

→ If you've recently tried to ignore that Still Small Voice – that *Call* to change – what is it trying to tell you?

→ What assumptions are you making that are stopping you acting upon it?

→ Who could help you take the first small steps on that journey of change?

→ When are you going to ask them for that help?

Chapter 5

Your Purpose: The Three Catalysts

Here we'll look at why business isn't just about winning clients, completing projects and delivering profits.

Here we'll look at the Three Catalysts that, when combined, **Ignite!** a business...

And so create, even in the smallest of firms, something that can only be described as Truly Great!

The Three Catalysts: What You Need to Know

There are Three Catalysts that tend to have the greatest capacity to set a business alight:

1. A Mission – we'll call this your *Passionate Purpose*
2. A Belief System – we'll call this your *Heartfelt Values*
3. A Difference – we'll call this your *Unique Abilities*

Yes, there are other catalysts, but these are the three that stand out for me.

Yet, even examining these Three Catalysts, there is one that I believe has the greatest **Power** to inspire and motivate: that catalyst is A Mission – or, in Soul Millionaire language, your Passionate Purpose.

I'll explain why.

Drawing upon a six-year research project at Stanford Graduate School of Business, Jim Collins and Jerry Porras studied 18 truly exceptional and long-lasting companies. Their study created the seminal book *Built to Last: Successful Habits of Visionary Companies.*

In that book you can find hundreds of specific examples, organised into a framework, showing what factors underpin so-called visionary companies.

See what they say about *Purpose:*

"The most financially successful companies are founded on solid values and belief systems. They have a higher purpose than just making money. Visionary companies go deeper and find the real reason for their being."

Collins and Porras conclude by saying:

"Pushed to choose between Core Purpose and Core Values, we would likely choose Core Purpose as the more important factor in guiding and inspiring an organisation."

We'll look at all Three Catalysts in this chapter. But, understanding your Passionate Purpose is likely to be the most powerful of the three in propelling you on The Soul Millionaire Journey.

Turn On The Light

By the end of the first phone call, I'd made it clear to Satnam that, using the politest of terms, I just wasn't interested in our working together.

You see, there are some organisations whose behaviour, ethos and culture go against the grain for me. The group Satnam was part of fitted that bill. And I wasn't prepared to invest time and energy paddling against that stream.

But he wouldn't let it rest there.

Effusively he went on about a *"vision"* that he had. He said, *"If you'll just let me show you a few pictures of it... I know you'll be interested."*

Eventually, I gave in. Crumbled. Capitulated. I suspected that I was going to regret doing so. But I had to admit that I was intrigued enough to peek into his "vision" and at his "pictures".

I set aside a morning, and we met at the Felbridge Hotel, near East Grinstead. It was the end of May, and the day was bright and hopeful.

Given a flipchart and pen, he went to work, babbling effusively about his vision, his dream.

Here was another *Wake Up, Alfie!* story.

He told me of a holiday that he'd taken with his family, visiting India.

He told me of the children he'd seen begging and groping – they were all blind, for one reason or another.

He told me what had gripped his soul before he'd stepped onto the plane to go home.

This is what he wanted to do...

"The most financially successful companies are founded on solid values and belief systems. They have a higher purpose than just making money."
Jim Collins & Jerry Porras

Satnam wanted to build a hospital in India. A hospital that would give children back their sight. Children who are part of the haunting statistic of blindness in that continent – eight million, blighted solely by cataracts.

Initially, my thoughts were, *I think this man is bonkers. Insane. How on earth is a financial planner, with only two staff, going to build a hospital?*

The problem (or more accurately, *my* problem) was, within 15 minutes I was hooked. My emotions wrestled with my business sense, as I became swept up by the ludicrous, beautiful, compassionate majesty of the idea.

He explained the timescale for his *ludicrous vision.*
In 12 years, he planned to build his business – and then sell it. This would create the multi-millions that the hospital project would need.

Hmmm. Possible, I thought.

I then asked him to sit down and pause for a moment. An idea was bubbling. One of those inklings that you get from time to time, with no apparent logic behind it.

"What if..." I asked. *"What if you could do that in, say, five years? What would that mean to you?"*

He grinned like a schoolboy being offered a bowl of chocolate ice cream.
"That would be amazing!" he enthused.

"Well, since I'm not interested in hanging around to see the results of this for 12 years," I continued, *"I propose we create a plan to fund this thing in five years maximum. That is, if you're up for the challenge?"*

And that was it. I was in.

Make It Real

Satnam's vision started to evolve from *wildly possible* to *wonderfully probable* and then to *glorious reality.* It became our mission, as we scribbled together, to give it substance and shape, resources and metrics.

On that day, we embarked upon the most unlikely of adventures. I committed to coaching him for up to five years, to Bring Light to One Million Children.

Now *that* is what I call a Passionate Purpose.

It's a **Purpose** that provides the energy and grittiness to overcome hurdles, obstacles and Exocet missiles that life (and people) will throw at any business.

How is Satnam's Passionate Purpose Progressing?

Well, at the time of writing, he's just entered the third year of our coaching journey together. Already, he's being thanked for saving the sight of dozens of children.

And he is in discussions with other business owners who are driven by a similar Passionate Purpose. Together, they're making what was once merely a *wildly possible* idea into a feet-on-the-ground *glorious reality:*

To Bring Light to One Million Children.

It's Time to Examine The Three Catalysts

Catalyst 1: Your Passionate Purpose

I've come to understand there are several levels to a Passionate Purpose:

→ **The first is unlike the SMART goals we learn about**
Most of us in business are relentlessly driven by tasks, goals and short-term strategies. Things that need to be achieved and fulfilled. Many haven't learned to mentally engage with something deeper, like Passionate Purpose – a concept that we cannot cross off our to-do list.

This level of Passionate Purpose is not a goal. It's like a guiding North Star: there to direct us, to inspire change in us, yet not necessarily to be reached.

However, once you have a sense of this Passionate Purpose, then you're ready to work on what Greg McKeown, in his book *Essentialism* calls your "essential intent". This intent takes a Passionate Purpose and makes it both concrete and measurable. So, for example, McKeown tells of Martha Lane Fox's appointment to the position of the first UK Digital Champion. Her essential intent was *"to get everyone in the UK online by the end of 2012"*. That's a concrete, and measurable, Passionate Purpose.

→ **On the other hand, beware of being too vague and shallow**
Teams become cynical (and disinterested) when leaders impose vague, inflated statements of Mission or Purpose.

Bland statements like "maximising shareholder value through service excellence and innovation" are about as useful as a chocolate teapot. Such statements lack clarity, motivate nobody and create confusion.

This level of Passionate Purpose will guide and inspire when it becomes both meaningful and memorable, measurable and concrete.

→ **It's to be uncovered, not discovered**

It's there, even if we don't recognise it, or know how to articulate it. It's been evolving ever since the business was founded. So, it's not a matter of *discovering*. It's more a matter of *uncovering*.

The problem is, once we do uncover it, many of us might find that our **Purpose** is not in the least inspiring – perhaps not even to ourselves.

→ **It's not about your Products or Service**

Your products or service will change and evolve and change again. They'll even be scrapped and replaced over a period of years.

Your Passionate Purpose, on the other hand, should be able to guide and inspire for the next 20 years or more.

→ **Few business leaders know how to capture and express it**

It's often said to me that men find it difficult to express what's deep in their heart – in their gut. Well, be that as it may, your Passionate Purpose is one of those things that *must* be felt in that way.

So, it's not surprising that many men, more accustomed to working with logic and metrics, then struggle to capture something so essentially emotional in their business life.

How then do you uncover your own Passionate Purpose, something that will *Ignite!* you – and those who engage with you – for years to come?

Great question!

To help you start thinking that through, I've provided some questions in the subheadings *What Did You Learn?* and *What Will You Do Now?* at the end of this chapter.

I recommend that you don't skip past those questions this time. The opportunity to think deeply about them will provide the basis on which much of your own Soul Millionaire Journey will be based.

So, don't sell yourself short!

"This is the true joy in life... being used for a purpose recognised by yourself as a mighty one. Being a force of Nature instead of a feverish little clod of self-importance, of ailments and grievances; complaining that the world will not devote itself to making you happy."

George Bernard Shaw

Make Allowance For Your Heroes

As we've already seen, Heroes often arise through ordinary mortals doing extraordinary things. But, being mortal, with finite perspective, sometimes they make mortal errors of judgment.

I recall one of my business Heroes making just such an error, even though he had extraordinary vision as a leader.

He had studied a business book and was sharing a little of it with me as we enjoyed lunch together. In doing so, he asked me a question:

"David, what would you say is the purpose of a business like ours – in fact, of any business?"

Hmmm.

I couldn't think quickly enough for him.

"Well, I'll tell you," he jumped in. *"It's this: to win and retain clients, and to do that at a profit."*

That was it.

To be honest, I was troubled. The statement hit me with all the earth-shattering force of a ball of cotton wool. I wasn't buying into it at all.

By the time I sat on the train for the exhausting commute home, I had worked out why. I mumbled to myself, *"Our cat drinks saucers of milk deeper than that statement!"*

Since that evening, everything I've learned about business has taught me that my instinct was right. Which is why I've reached this conclusion: to say that the **Purpose** of business is to make a profit is like saying, *"The **Purpose** of life is to breathe in and out."*

Of course, we'd struggle to get through more than a few seconds of life if we didn't breathe in and out! But a **Purpose** for our life? Really?

We who lead businesses can do better than that in our thinking. We must do better than that.

Uncover What's Already There

I vividly remember one Managing Director staring at me and saying, *"But I don't know what my purpose is! I don't think I have one. I know that I need to make a profit in business. But I haven't a clue what my purpose is in life."*

Now, this would be normal for our first coaching conversation. Asking someone about their Passionate Purpose in life is not a typical topic for casual conversation. But this was one of many discussions over a period of nine months. He was still struggling, with the *why* of his life.

I reminded him of our first meeting, when, in tears, he had described his life as feeling "empty", even though others envied his income and possessions.

I left this message with him, before concluding our relationship:

"Frankly, if, at the end of your days, you don't know the answer to this 'why' question of your life... it will matter very little what else you do know."

> To say that the purpose of business is to make a profit is like saying that the purpose of life is to breathe in and out.

Let's Listen to Mary Again

Remember Mary from the beginning of this Journey?

She was driven by a Passionate Purpose, the seeds of which were planted in childhood. Decades later, this has blossomed into a business model and service that goes well beyond merely helping women to understand and organise their money.

What Mary's work with clients does is to create calm out of chaos, peace out of pandemonium, healing out of heartache.

Mary's Passionate Purpose helped in her marketing too.

When first meeting with 12 different teams of solicitors specialising in helping women in the throes of divorce, she found that she didn't need to sell her expertise.

She viewed each of those meetings through the lens of her Passionate Purpose. This made her sensitive to any of their comments that could guide her in designing a completely new, more relevant, service.

It was an approach to business that was rare, engaging, memorable. Certainly, those solicitors felt so, and they championed her services.

Commercially, embracing her Passionate Purpose has allowed Mary to create a minimum fee structure which is five times the industry average. And an Elite Service Fee three times that.

More importantly, her reputation has freed her to live the more relaxed life that she yearned for.

Being guided by a Passionate Purpose does that to a person. And to a company.

> "Frankly, if, at the end of your days, you don't know the answer to this WHY question of your life... it will matter very little what else you do know."

Give it Time

In the early years of our business, we can be forgiven for focusing on getting clients and revenue through the door.

At this stage, articulating our Passionate Purpose might seem somewhat academic – however overwhelming the evidence of its impact.

Even some of the Visionary Companies we read about found that their Passionate Purpose was strongly felt throughout its culture. It was there – just not overtly spoken about.

Indeed, even after coaching some clients for many months, they still wrestle with this fundamental principle. So, don't feel that you need to panic.

It's foundational. But it's just one factor on the journey. One factor in lifting your business to the level of Extraordinary. Remember, there are a number of major blocks to any foundation. Perhaps we can call this *The Corner Stone.*

I wonder. **Maybe, after reading this chapter, your Purpose is to find your Passionate Purpose!**

Catalyst 2: Your Heartfelt Values

Leaders often confuse **Values** with **Purpose.**

Yes, there's a strong correlation between the two. However, it's important to recognise that they are different, and that they act as complementary Catalysts in the driving force of a business.

Your Passionate Purpose defines *why* you, your business or your team, even exist.

Your Heartfelt Values, on the other hand, define *what* you believe in, what you stand for, and what you're prepared to stand up and fight for.

In Martin Luther King Jr. terms, they're what you're prepared to *die* for.

> *"Great businesses have a point of view, not just a product or service. You have to believe in something. You need to know what you're willing to fight for."*
> **Jason Fried and David Hansson**

The question is: how does an individual or a team go about the task of defining what they really value?

Use These Three Simple Steps

I've found it helpful to use the approach taken by Gino Wickman in his excellent book *Traction:*

Step one
List *three* people who, if you could create their avatar, would lead your firm to domination in your selected market.

(For example, a couple of my workshop delegates immediately pounced on the name Sir David Brailsford. The man who led Team GB's cycling squad from *one* Olympic gold medal in 2000 to *twelve* Olympic medals in 2016.)

Step two

List *at least* seven characteristics that these people embody, asking yourself:

→   What seven qualities do they exemplify?
→   What do they do that brings them onto your radar?

For example, do they:

→   Continually strive for perfection?
→   Serve first, eat last?
→   Demonstrate courage with humility?
→   Do the right thing?
→   Encourage and reward teamwork?
→   Engage in lifelong learning?

Step three

The above exercise is likely to have created a long list, right?

So now you have to select just three qualities or characteristics, that you feel are truly, truly important. Lots is easy. Less is difficult.

But, as is often the case, less is definitely more.

Invest Your Courage

Focusing your attention on an individual's character is a step towards understanding what those individuals truly value. Add to that their consistent behaviour over time, and this tends to reveal what they stand for and believe in.

Your Heartfelt Values are not characteristics that you spend energy justifying to others. They're what you believe in, deep in the very gut of your being, and in the core of your organisation.

What's more you don't change your Heartfelt Values to fit the changing market or your clients' changing views. You change your market (or clients) in order to remain true to your Heartfelt Values!

"Inspired employees who find meaning in their organisation's purpose and values are 1.5 x more productive than when simply engaged, and 2.25 x more productive than when simply satisfied."

Bain & Co

If you invest your courage in holding to those Heartfelt Values they'll start to shape your world. Together with your Passionate Purpose, they'll act as a dual lens in every business decision you'll now make.

Through this filter, you'll learn to accept or discard ideas, advice – even clients and potential new recruits.

(For an expression of this, see Figure 5, p.111.)

Be in no doubt about the price our businesses pay, and the problems we create for ourselves – when we're not clear about our own Heartfelt Values. Perhaps we've never even considered the concept.

Firstly, we develop organisations that are two-dimensional, mechanical and bland. With nothing more meaningful to fuel their interest, a team centres its attention on obvious metrics such as numbers of clients, recurrent revenue and profit margin.

Next, you'll attract the kind of team members, and the kind of clients, who also think in this two-dimensional way about business and life.

By choosing to stand for... well, very little at all... you're unwittingly choosing to be Value-less. And that's what your business will portray to the world.

Whilst that does mean that there's nothing for people to dislike or reject, it also means that there's absolutely nothing for them to get excited about.

Catalyst 3: Your Unique Abilities

It's true that the idea of Unique Abilities, sometimes called *Unique Service Proposition* (USP), is not a concept that immediately lends itself to the financial services community. The history of the community over the last 30 years has made sure of that, because of habits like those below:

→ **Product** providers have churned out sales teams nurtured with the same mindsets and mantras.

→ These sales teams have left these product providers and gone on to form the foundation of today's financial advisory community.

→ In turn, top revenue performers were, and still are, paraded as people that others should emulate.

→ Then, best-practice meetings encouraged everyone to feel that, if they just copied top performers, we might all manage to enjoy the same level of commercial success.

For many decades, very little emerged from this sector that we – or more importantly, the public – could portray as unusual, certainly not *unique.*

However, I do observe that this sector – perhaps responding to regulation and changing consumer expectations – has started to create leaders whose thinking is breaking with the past.

Moreover, I do believe that it's now possible to create a business that is notably *different* to others within this sector. Not only is it possible. I'm convinced that it's becoming increasingly essential.

I recall first glancing at the title of Jack Trout's book on marketing, *Differentiate or Die*, and initially thinking, *Hmmm, isn't that title just a little extreme? Will a company really die, just because they don't differentiate themselves clearly from their competitors?*

However, seeing the number of firms that continue sailing blissfully in the grip of mediocrity – and towards a long, slow demise – I'm now more convinced that Trout was making an important point.

I'm becoming a believer in this simple, but elusive, idea. Differences, your Unique Abilities, are a crucial element in being able to *Ignite!* a business.

Seizing a different idea, dramatising it, making it your own – these are ways to carve out your unique space in an overcrowded marketplace. Those who master this approach can expect significant reward for their courage.

Of course, the question arises: *What exactly is so different about my firm?*
And, if the answer is "very little at all" then how do I change that?

Since the impact of getting this right is so considerable, allow me to share:

→   Some simple principles
→   One or two examples

How to Be Different, Even Unique

When meeting a firm for the first time, what I look for is an unusual combination of factors. Is there a set of skills, behaviours, services, client types, location, whatever, that – when combined – could distinguish this organisation from others around it? I call this a Unique Combination.

If not yet, then could there be a Unique Combination for you, within one to three years – given new thinking and behaviour?

Let's look at some possible components that could create such Unique Combinations:

→ **Location**
You probably prefer working with clients in a particular location: say, within a 20-mile radius of your office.

→ **Client Type**
If you're commercially savvy, you've come to realise that focusing your resources towards a very specific type of client pays huge dividends, both tangible and intangible.

→ **Skillset**
Rather than be a generalist, you might have discovered that clients pay far more attention to those whom they regard as experts at something.

→ **Services**
You might have designed services that best serve a particular type of client. Or they are delivered in a way that never ceases to delight new and existing clients.

You get the idea. And I'm sure that there are other components I've missed that are obvious to you. Now, what would happen if you carefully combined some of those components into a Unique Combination of your own?

Let's create a couple of examples:

Unique Combination A

→ **Location**
You're based in Hertfordshire.
→ **Client Type**
You seem to work best with highly-paid female executives.
→ **Skillset**
You've become skilled in helping them map out a financial structure which could underpin their exit strategy from exhausting, stressful roles.
→ **Services**
You've created alliances with an executive coach and an adventure and expedition specialist – professionals who can help them rethink their life, and open their mind to new possibilities.

Unique Combination B

→ **Location**
You're based in the Thames Valley.
→ **Client Type**
You seem to work best with founders of high-tech businesses.

→ **Skillset**

You've become skilled in helping them to financially underpin the next five to ten years of their life, which is currently consumed with daily business demands.

→ **Services**

You've created alliances with an exit consultant and a team of business angels. Together, you have the Unique Combination of skills for them to resurrect dreams and aspirations long buried in the striving for success.

Finally, let's look at an example you've already met in earlier chapters:

Unique Combination C

→ **Location**

You're based in Surrey.

→ **Client Type**

Women in the early stages of divorce.

→ **Skillset**

You've developed professional coaching skills which, when combined with financial planning skills, provide an unusual level of empathy, support and clarity.

→ **Services**

Your coordinating work with divorce lawyers, with legal coaches, with life coaches, all combine to provide a support network that is unique in the south-east of England.

It's Your Turn to Stand Out And Be Unique

Let's look at your business.

→   Consider the factors below (and others that come to mind).
→   Comment on each of them,
→   Then stand back and see if what you've created is a possible Unique Combination:

→   **Location**

_____

_____

_____

_____

→   **Client Type**

_____

_____

_____

_____

→   **Skillset**

_____

_____

_____

_____

→   **Services**

_____

_____

_____

_____

Set Yourself Free

Most small to medium size firms (SMEs) suffer from what is commonly termed _founder's syndrome._ This means:

→   The business is strongly identified with the founder.
→   The majority of important decisions flow from this founder.

→ There is no formal process to gain input from others on important decisions.

→ There is no agreed succession plan.

→ Key staff are selected to support the founder, not to fulfil the business' Passionate Purpose.

→ The founder and leader seems to have an unusual set of qualities that magnetically attracts the best, highest-paying clients.

→ The founder is unusually skilled at handling the most complex client relationships.

→ The majority of the revenue stems from the founder's efforts.

→ The founder finds it very, very difficult to let go of the reins to employees.

This is the culture created by most charismatic personalities. That culture has become known as *The Genius with 1,000 Little Helpers.*

You'll find this discussed in Jim Collins' book *Good To Great.* The term pops up again in Dr Carol Dweck's book *Mindset.*

Dweck's comment was that such leaders never did build extraordinary organisations like Jim Collins' *Good To Great* companies.

Instead, *"They operate on a 'fixed-mindset' that Great Geniuses (like themselves) do not need great teams. They just need little helpers to carry out their brilliant ideas."*

However, when the business, the team, become clear about their Three Catalysts (let me remind you):

THE FLIGHT OF THE SOUL MILLIONAIRE

→ Passionate Purpose
→ Heartfelt Values
→ Unique Abilities...

... those three factors – not The Genius – start to become the glue that holds the business together. The business starts to have a Soul of its own. A Soul Millionaire business is created that is:

→ **Sustainable**
   It starts to become sustainable, without the founder.
→ **Scaleable**
   It has a chance of becoming scaleable in size – up or down.
→ **Saleable**
   In the eyes of astute, acquisitive organisations, the business takes on a much higher saleable value.

The business, and the founder, start to become *free.*

"It's not what you believe that sets you apart... so much as the fact that you believe in something... that you believe in it deeply... that you bring it to life."
Jim Collins & Jerry Porras

Figure 5

| Hire | Fire | Review | Recognise | Reward |

| Create | Engage | Serve |

| Learn | Lead | Legacy |

Passionate Purpose
Heartfelt Values
Unique Abilities

The Future You're Creating

→ The first line is about how you work with your team

→ The second line is about how you create and serve new clients

→ The third line is about how you lead your organisation.

The Thinking Bench

Chesley Burnett 'Sully' Sullenberger III became a national hero, as a result of landing US Airways Flight 1549 on the Hudson River, on 15th January 2009.

With both engines suddenly disabled by a passing flock of geese, and no way to reach the nearest airport, logic dictated that it was impossible to land the Airbus safely – anywhere!

Yet all 155 passengers survived.

In spite of this modern-day miracle, Sully came under investigation for pilot error.

Why?

Because some computer simulations said that he should have tried for LaGuardia airport. He stood to lose his career, pension rights, reputation – everything.

Thankfully, the flight recording and the salvaged, shattered engines finally proved the simulations wrong.

In the film, *Sully*, one of those chairing the public hearing said this:

"I can say with absolute confidence that, after speaking with the rest of the flight crew... with bird experts, aviation engineers...

After running through every scenario, after interviewing each player... there is still an "x" in this result. And it is you, Captain Sullenberger.

Remove you from the equation, and the maths just fails."

When we study the factors that help any business to own a unique position in the hearts and minds of (potential) clients, there is always one factor which is far from logical.

That factor is *you:*

→ The unique journey that only you have travelled.
→ The person you've become, as a result of that journey.
→ The person you're intentionally becoming.

We bring our humanity to our work, whether we believe it, recognise it or like it.

Who you are and what you've become, your story, is part of the uniqueness in your business.

Everybody has a story.

When I was about to publish mine, I was embarrassed.
I thought that it wasn't worth reading about.
It now seems that I was the only person who thought that.

Let the world know about your story.
They might decide they like what they hear.

What Have You Learned?

→   What do you believe is the main **Purpose** for your life on this earth?
→   How have you come to that conclusion or feeling?
→   What relationships do you value most?
→   What beliefs and values determine how you reach decisions?
→   As you ponder your life, what have you found that most inspires you?
→   What does your heart, your experience, and feedback from others, teach you are your most distinct talents?
→   How different do these distinct talents cause you to be from your peers?

→ How are your differences and strengths woven into your business?

→ As you look at the answer to all of these questions, how do they meet a significant need in this world?

What Will You Do Now?

→ In reviewing the dreams and aspirations you had, perhaps just three years ago, where are you on that journey?

→ Where have you written the detail of your Passionate Purpose (in life and business), your Heartfelt Values and your Unique Abilities?

→ Apart from you, who knows about those three aspects of your business?

→ What will you do to ensure that all the people who should know, do know? And when will you start to do that?

Chapter **6**

People

The term **People** can apply both internally and externally during The Soul Millionaire Journey.

On the one hand, they're the kind of people you want to build into an extraordinary team. On the other they are the kind of people you desire as clients.

Here, we'll concentrate on the surprising results gained by being far more selective about the kind of **clients** you serve.

1. The Awakening, Call & Refusal		Purpose
	Ignite!	
2. The Teacher Appears		People

3. Mission Preparation		Preparation
	Engage!	
4. Crosses to New World		Pioneering

5. Friendships & Opposition		Possibility
	Inspire!	
6. The Wilderness Test		Power

7. Final Test, Reward, Travel Home		Prosperity
	Elevate!	
8. The New Mission		Posterity

Look at The Numbers

The memory of that King's Cross attic office of yesterday returns to haunt me like the Ghost of Times Past whenever I find myself lacking gratitude today.

It was a cold, miserable place in the winter. Wearing gloves at my desk was not unusual. In summer, my head ached as I sweated and suffocated. Thankfully, I only 'served' one year there.

The people I was surrounded by were no less inclement: seeming both heartless and self-serving. What I saw in their behaviour with clients horrified me.

What a terrible, rushed decision I had made in escaping from a local firm on the borders of Surrey, supposedly trying to improve the ethics of my environment.

More crushing was the thought that I couldn't recall a single enjoyable week of the two years I'd spent as a product-focused financial adviser.

I was exhausted, constantly ill, never at home, and ready to admit my failure. I made plans to leave the financial services sector and try a 'proper' career.

Then... one single conversation in Windmill Street lifted my spirits, changed my mind and redirected my business future.

I had a chance meeting with an old colleague – Doug Woodward, Managing Director of a successful IT recruitment company based in London's West End.

In my earlier career – in IT recruitment – I'd trained him as a young recruitment consultant. He proved an exceptional, talented spirit, with boundless energy and daring. Within a decade he was on his way to leading the country's premier organisation in its sector.

What I learned from Doug was my most valuable lesson in marketing strategy – I just didn't recognise that at the time.

"Why not focus on one type of client?" he prompted. *"I'll introduce you to some of ours. Obviously, they're all software consultants: tiny businesses, and with no idea about how to replace their previous employment benefits."*

He was true to his word.

Within six months, I had enough money to employ a PA/administrator, plus some (very) basic office technology (remember daisy-wheel printers?).

Within 12 months, we'd moved from that miserable attic to serviced offices in Moorgate, where I joined forces with a church friend. For a time, he became a mentor and anchor in my life.

Within 18 months, my specialist knowledge of the IT sector had boosted our reputation amongst a dozen recruitment firms. They asked us to supply brochures for their sales consultants to hand out.

And the referrals started flowing.

Within 24 months, we were receiving a minimum of two referrals every week from those firms – every week!

As a result, we moved to the first floor of (what was then) Western Australia House on The Strand, and expanded our team to four advisers, with matching support staff.

Less is More

My business education was well under way. **And the most obvious, and stark, lesson I'd learned was this:** when it came to attracting and serving clients, *narrowing* our focus had led to *expanding:*

→   Our opportunities.
→   Our reputation.
→   Our evangelists.
→   Our referrals.
→   Our financial results.

The numbers were extraordinary. The numbers were consistent. The numbers didn't lie.

However, looking back, it took 20 years to fully understand all the factors – the *whys* – that combined to create those numbers and that success. I'll share those factors with you – later.

Read The Reports, You Might Be Wrong

In any business sector, building reputation and trust is paramount.

So, it's not surprising that business leaders and their teams feel justifiably proud when they can point to referrals and introductions as their main source of new clients.

What's even more noteworthy is when the bulk of those referrals are precisely the type of clients that firms would consider their ideal. These Ideal Clients, or *avatars* as some like to call them, represent the top 20 percent of clients that actually create 80 percent of your revenue, fulfilment and enjoyment. Whereas the other 80 percent do none of that; instead generating activity that drains time and resources.

Think of the time, money and energy saved on frenetic marketing activity when Ideal Client referrals flow steadily into your business!

Given the importance of gaining referrals, it makes sense that it has been the subject of a multitude of books, seminars and courses, particularly in the small business sector. Financial Services is no exception to the desire for this information.

I've studied much of this material over the years. But nothing prepared me for what I came across in 2011. In that year I read a report written by Julie Littlechild, founder of Adviser Impact and now CEO of AbsoluteEngagement.com.

It was a revelation.

| Advisers' assumptions about what clients wanted and valued about their services were often at odds with what **clients** said they wanted and valued.

This report caused me to realise that much of what I'd previously studied was based on anecdotes, assumptions and subjective views. And, to misquote John Anderson of SEI, *"The plural of 'story' is not 'data'. Nor is the plural of 'anecdote' spelled 'empirical evidence'."*

Most importantly, Julie's team of professional researchers found that advisers' assumptions about what clients wanted and valued about their services were often at odds with what *clients* said they wanted and valued.

This was interesting, to say the least.

With Julie's initial report we finally had clear empirical evidence of an elusive question: *"Why do clients feel so deeply engaged with a firm that they are happy to provide appropriate referrals?"*

On the one hand, Julie's research dispelled many popular and pleasing myths that have flowed unchecked from one 'best-practice meeting' to another.

On the other, her reports mapped out decisions and behaviours that firms must undertake to create deeply-engaged clients and professional connections, who will act as that firm's ardent evangelists.

One of those decisions is to direct the firm's attention to serving a particular type of client: your Ideal Client.

Since that report, which I read in 2011, Julie has continued her research, together with other consultants like Steve Wershing, CFP® (President, The Client Driven Practice). The results have strengthened and augmented her original conclusions.

Focusing your attention on serving your Ideal Client – a very particular type of client – pays significant and measurable dividends. The benefits are felt by both the advisory firm and their clients.

What's Stopping Them?

If the evidence is so overwhelming (and it is), why is it that so few leaders of financial planning firms commit to focusing their attention in this way?

I've been listening carefully, over a period of 10 years, to try and understand the answers to that question.

I've arrived at a few observations:

→ **They're scared of missing opportunities.**
The logic seems to be that if they focused on saying "yes" to a particular type of prospective client, then they'd lose revenue by saying "no" to prospective clients who don't fit the criteria.

→ **They're determined to serve everybody.**
The argument here is that they feel uncomfortable being 'elitist' in their work.
They believe that everybody deserves to have financial advice... so why would they turn anybody away?

→ **Their business would be vulnerable concentrating on one type of client.**
They point to the **Possibility** that concentrating on dentists, for example, might weaken their future. They point to the wave of dental practices being swallowed up by large brands in this decade, leading to a sea-change in the fortunes of dentists.

→ **Just as important, they fear that other professionals –**
potential introducers and centres of influence – would see them as 'cherry picking' and find that unpalatable.

→ **They're frightened that there won't be sufficient opportunities in the niche they choose.**
They ask, *"What if I thought of dealing with vets, but then found there weren't many vets in my area of the country?"*

→ **They fear offending existing clients.**
They fear that clients might become upset when they see that they don't fit the new Ideal Client description.

→ **They simply don't know how to select a specific client type.**
How are they supposed to know what specific client type would work best for them?

What's clear is that all of these concerns are based on:

→ Fear
→ Uncertainty
→ Lack of knowledge.

Creating a business and service which you hope many people will LIKE... is an excellent way of creating something which not enough people will passionately LOVE.

Shatter Your Fear And Uncertainty With The Why

Behind this fear and uncertainty sit a number of assumptions that colour and distort the facts.

The easiest way to shatter these assumptions is to examine the evidence – the truth – that emerges from both research and practice-in-the-field.

Let's first look at the *outcomes* – the demonstrable results – of selecting a very specific Ideal Client. Doing so will allow you to see *why* this approach is well supported by crushing logic.

Experience – and research – show that focusing your attention on a specific type of Ideal Client makes your life, and your clients' lives, *easier.*

Ten Reasons Why This Focus Makes Life Easier and More Fulfilling

Yes, that's right, there are ten reasons, at least:

1. **It's easier...** to learn about, understand and empathise with the world, the language and the problems of prospective Ideal Clients if those clients are of a very similar type.

2. **It's easier...** to create messages and case studies (online or offline, verbally or in writing) that grab the attention of, and resonate with, prospective Ideal Clients.

3. **It's easier...** to define what your Ideal Client values. This is because different types of client (naturally) value different things. (More on this later.)

4. **It's easier...** to design and deliver services that meet what your Ideal Client really, really values, rather than what you wish them to value.

5. **It's easier...** to charge much higher fees, since the way that you (and your team) are serving the client is perfectly relevant and supremely tailored to their needs.

6. **It's easier...** to construct systems and processes tailored to meet the expectations of your Ideal Client, which is part of what they see as 'value'.

7. **It's easier...** to gain a reputation as an expert, when it is clear to everybody that you are highly knowledgeable in serving a particular community. Good news spreads faster in closer-knit communities.

8. **It's easier...** for clients to spot a colleague, friend or family member who could best be served by you; the client knows exactly who you serve best.

9. **It's easier…** to develop relationships with introducers who are also knowledgeable about that niche market.
10. **It's easier…** to keep your client at the very heart of everything, rather than focus your attention on selling a service that you hope all and sundry will fall in love with.

This focus just makes life easier!

Fear and uncertainty are strong emotional forces. They've certainly been at the heart of limiting opportunities for thousands of professionals in your sector.

But I hope you can now see that knowledge, understanding and courageous action are strong antidotes, and excellent companions in your journey to a better future.

Perhaps the best way to capture this principle of focus is to say: *"Creating a business and a service that you hope many people will **like**… is an excellent way to create something that not enough people will passionately **love**."*

And, as marketing consultant Seth Godin points out: *"Our best work can't possibly appeal to the average masses."*

Firstly, you can't work with the masses anyway! You have a limit on your time and capacity.

More importantly, you're there to build something that people will hunt for, that people will talk about. Something that those who love that *something* will clamour for and be excited by… and pay well over the odds to be a part of. But it'll be something that's not for everyone.

When they see and hear your messages, they must know immediately that you're talking specifically to them. Otherwise you're seen as talking to everybody. Ask yourself: *do **you** want to be treated like you're merely everybody else?*

It's almost time to answer that question above: *"How do I select a specific client type that works best for me and my firm?"*

One more point before we do.

Before we Discuss The How... Let's Talk About Value

Business language, just like everyday conversational language, is forever developing. Fads and fashions develop into jargon – often meaningless, frequently ostentatious, sometimes downright silly.

One of the hackneyed phrases that has emerged in very recent years, particularly in financial services, is the word *proposition.*

Something that used to be simply *our service* has now evolved into *our client proposition, our service proposition or our value proposition.*

The problem with assumptive language, like *value proposition,* is that it leads us to believe what we're proposing will, of course, be valuable to our prospective client.

Such an assumption isn't helpful – to either the client or to your business.

There are two reasons behind me speaking so bluntly:

1. **I would suggest that *value* doesn't reside within our service or Product.**
   Surely, *value* resides firmly within the mind and heart of our existing and future Ideal Client.
2. **Each type of Ideal Client, each niche market, values different approaches and services in order to meet their distinctly different needs.**
   Which means that... your specific type of Ideal Client, the niche market you're targeting... defines *value* – not you!
   For example...
   I'm hard pushed to believe that a 52-year-old lady, newly widowed, would value the same kind of messages, conversation, understanding, skills and services... as a 45-year-old Managing Director of a £5 million turnover, light engineering company.
   That simply doesn't make sense to me.
   And I'm not sure it makes sense to you, either.

> When they see and hear your messages, they must know immediately that you're talking specifically to **them.**

The Four Quadrants

As you can see, the arguments for taking this more focused route are strong.

The question is: *how* do you make such a clear decision?

→ How do you decide which type of Ideal Client you'd love to work with?

→ How do you decide which type of Ideal Client you and your firm are predisposed to work best with?

→ How do you decide what messages and services would be most attractive to that type of Ideal Client?

→ How do you understand what they really, really want from a service like yours?

How?

Well, I'll show you how.

What's essential when trying to describe your Ideal Client is to define them with crystal clarity.

The vaguer you are in doing this, the less chance you have of being heard above the cacophony of marketing messages bombarding them every day of their lives.

What I normally do when explaining this to an audience is to draw one of those Boston Matrix graphics. You know, a two-by-two matrix with four quadrants (see Figure 6, p.137).

The Four Quadrants are as follows:

Quadrant 1: Demography and Community

This answers the question: *"What does the Ideal Client look like?"*

Demography?

Think like a government actuary: age... marital status... gender... children... location... sexuality... ethnic background... religion... income... assets... and so on.

(Please note: there's no room here for dancing around with pointless and stultifying concepts like political correctness. This is about whom *you* and your team wish to spend your working life serving. That's *your* choice, and *your* choice alone.)

Community?

Within that demographic, ask this question: is my Ideal Client easily identified as being part of a particular community?

This could be a specific business community – such as an executive role within a specific profession or commercial sector.

Or it could be a life/lifestyle community (such as widows, divorcees and so forth).

Keep in mind that focusing on a particular community is only helpful if that makes it easier to reach your Ideal Client.

Quadrant 2: Psychography

This answers the question: *"What does the Ideal Client think or feel?"*

You might ask, *"Think or feel about what?"*
Good question.

Well, it's certainly easier to spend years working with a client whose value system is not diametrically opposed to yours.

But what sets apart brilliant marketing from the mediocre is when organisations are in tune with the lifestyle, attitude and buying preferences of their target markets.

They ask: *"When it comes to buying this type of product or service, what do we **want** this audience to be thinking or feeling as they make a buying decision?"*

Think of some of the brands you see advertising perfumes at Christmas. The messages are laser-beam directed towards a particular age and lifestyle: the characters and surroundings in a Dior advert look completely different to those in, for example, a Calvin Klein advert.

You need to write down very clearly what you want *your* Ideal Client to be thinking and feeling when they consider your firm.

Quadrant 3: Painful Problems

This answers the question: *"What painful problem is the Ideal Client wrestling with right now?"*

I wish that I'd coined the following quote. I'm not even sure where it came from; I've been using it for so many years:

"If you are able to articulate my problems better than I can (and perhaps before we've even met), then two things happen between you and me:

1. *You have my attention;*
2. *I inherently believe that you probably possess the solution to my problem."*

In practice, I – and countless others – have found the above quote to be true. Always.

Your ability to articulate the kind of problems that your Ideal Client community is typically wrestling with... well, that ability is **priceless.** Because:

→   It will gain the attention of your desired audience.
→   It will start to engender trust.
→   It will make you relevant in their eyes.

Be aware that the typical problems in your Ideal Client's life might not be directly related to your service or **Product.**

For example, I once asked 25 delegates at a workshop for financial planners to list the problems of a 48-year-old director of an IT systems company. Male, married, two children.

They identified 48 likely problems. Only eight of these were about money!

The point did not escape their notice.

Quadrant 4: Desired Outcomes

This answers the question: *"What would the Ideal Client really, really love to happen in their life, as a result of working with you and your firm?"*

Note: this is about what happens in your Ideal Client's *life*. Not necessarily what happens to their *money*.

Which begs the question: *"What sort of outcomes will your clients enjoy by working with you?"*

Before you answer that, it's important to recognise the marked difference between two types of outcomes:

1. Tangible, and
2. Intangible.

Why is this so important?

... because each type of outcome has a different commercial (and therefore measurable) impact on your relationship with your client.

So, what is a Tangible Outcome?

It's easier to answer this by looking at appropriate synonyms. For example, a Tangible Outcome is:

→ External to the person, that is, it's not normally something happening inside them.
→ Measurable and/or
→ Visible and/or
→ Physically touchable.

An example might be: *"Mrs Client, taking the action outlined in our financial plan will allow you to retire four years earlier than you'd originally anticipated."*

Four years is definitely measurable = Tangible.

What, then, is an Intangible Outcome?

Not surprisingly we can use the opposite synonyms to those used for Tangible.
For example, an Intangible Outcome is:

→ Internal to the person and/or
→ Not measurable and/or
→ Not visible and/or
→ Not physically touchable.

An example might be: *"Mr and Mrs Client, now you can enjoy the peace of mind and security you previously lacked. Your financial affairs are carefully organised to support your aspirations and dreams. You can relax in the knowledge that those things most important to you will indeed happen."*

My experience teaches me that it is clearly-defined, Intangible Outcomes that have the deepest and longest-lasting impact on your relationship with your client. What's more, they'll pay you far more for them, and for far longer.

Now that you're clear about who you want to serve...
Now that you've applied some science and research to the people you're going to spend thousands of hours serving in the coming years...

It's time to learn how to help them engage proactively and excitedly with your business.

It's time to spread your wings a little, as you prepare to fly.

Figure 6

Demography	Psychography
Problems	Outcomes

The Thinking Bench

I've conducted coaching conversations in some lovely, inspiring settings: country clubs, golf clubs, spas, mansions.

But few locations have been as surprising as overlooking the beach in front of Jamie Oliver's Fifteen Cornwall restaurant at Watergate Bay. It was October, and we were watching the surfers, whilst lounging in our shirtsleeves.

At first, I'd declined to travel to Cornwall for an exploratory meeting – no matter what the fee. But Wendy encouraged me, with these words: *"Don't be so stuffy! Get away from your office. You know how much you love Cornwall."*

So, here I was with Simon, seeing if we could speed the growth of his young business, and wondering whether this really was work, or just a jaunt.

Fifteen months later, his recurrent revenue had grown by 500 percent. His flow of referrals kept him fully occupied and with no time for any form of marketing other than simply talking to the right people in the right locations.

How did he do it? By carefully analysing the demographic factors (age, marital status, employment status, location, source of introduction...) of his current client community. He then focused hard on married couples where the oldest partner was between the age of 55 and 72.

Oh, and he reduced his travel around six counties, to focus more on the two counties from which flowed exactly 80 percent of his recurrent revenue.

It wasn't 'rocket'. But it was a simple science.
And it took great courage for a small, recently formed business to say *"No!"* to those who regularly approached this charming man.

The concept of the Ideal Client can make life so much more enjoyable.

THE FLIGHT OF THE SOUL MILLIONAIRE

What Have You Learned?

→ How specific and clearly defined is the description of your Ideal Client?

→ Which of the six reasons I've mentioned have stopped you being so specific and clear?

→ What proactive, planned, coherent strategy have you put in place to create referral opportunities?

→ Have you read any of the reports created by Julie Littlechild, Steve Wershing, CFP®, or John Anderson regarding engaging clients or creating referrals?

→ Which of the 10 *Easier* reasons (for being more specific about your Ideal Client) most appeals to you?

→ What research and evidence points to the *value* in your value proposition?

What Will You Do Now?

→ Which of the Four Quadrants (demography & community, psychography, painful problems, desired outcomes) would you prefer to guide your Ideal Client description?

→ What's behind that choice?

→ What does a close analysis of your existing client community tell you about:
  ⇨ Which type of clients you prefer?
  ⇨ Which type of clients prefer you?
  ⇨ ...and which provides your business with the greatest commercial rewards?

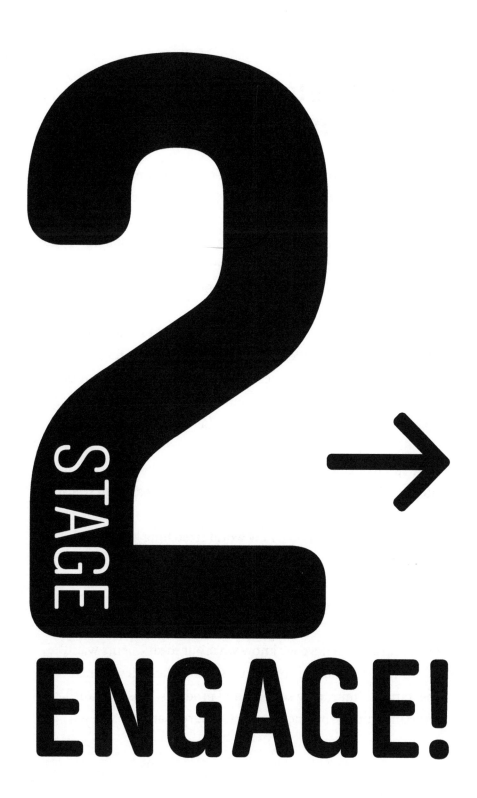

2

STAGE

ENGAGE!

What You Need to Know About The Engage! Stage

As in any of life's journeys there are stages and milestones that need to be mapped out. There is Preparation to be done.

This applies whether ascending Everest or carving out a new route across the Antarctic. It applies whether you're a struggling business, or already successful and a leading brand in your field.

Even the most daring, accomplished and fabled **Pioneers** invested time, energy and resources in careful **Preparation** before embarking on life-questioning adventures – crossing into an Unknown World. When they didn't, when they became casual or careless, they tended to pay a heavy price; sometimes with their lives.

As the speed of global change throws businesses into new white-water rapids of competition, the principles of **Preparation** still apply.

Each year seems to herald a new world stretching before us. Consequently, resting on the laurels of our previous success, falling in love with our own reputation, can blind us into thinking that research, **Preparation** and planning is for novices.

For example, we believe we know what our Ideal Clients want, but our Ideal Clients are constantly shifting their views and expectations. Innovative services and products, plus brilliant marketing from all business sectors, ensure that shift.

Which means that what got you *here* today, is unlikely to get you *there* tomorrow.

What the *Engage!* stage does is to help you **Prepare** those strengths and capabilities you'll need to negotiate this ever-changing world.

The *Engage!* stage examines the capabilities you'll need for:

1. **Preparation**
   You'll learn how to engage current and potential clients (and those who can give you access to them) in the kinds of conversations that will arm you with rare insights.
   This is where you learn to build upon the process of Client Engagement: the process that started when you committed to only seeking The Right Clients for your business. Now you'll start to learn the use of The Right Questions, to engage those clients – and their trust – more quickly, more purposefully.
   In doing so, you'll uncover what clients, potential clients and the influencers in their market really, really want – rather than what they first tell you they want.
2. **Pioneering**
   You'll develop skills and take actions that will mark you out from the crowd.
   You'll be doing what others dare not do – and you'll be loving it. You'll expect to be questioned – even criticised and railed against – but, notably, not by your clients. Launching further into The Soul Millionaire Journey, you'll be different, so expect your Pioneering to unsettle your colleagues and your peers. Change agents have always created such a response.

We'll use this Spirit of Pioneering to influence the three stages that naturally follow the Preparation you've invested in. We'll call these three stages:

i.   **Positioning**
ii. **Pricing**
iii. **Product**

By **Positioning,** we mean the messages communicated by what you do, say or write to your Ideal Client market. This will be informed by what you've discovered in your **Preparation.**

By **Product,** we mean the magnetic, relevant, make-a-difference service you'll create once you've done your homework about what your Ideal Client market really, really wants.

By **Pricing,** we mean setting fees that reflect the wisdom, knowledge, skills, time and energy you're bringing into play to serve your client. But, far more importantly, fees that reflect how much your clients value your extraordinary and relevant service in their lives.

All of this, because you're clear what relevant means, from your **Preparation.**

We'll Also Tackle The Why And How of Engagement

What will also emerge from the *Engage!* stage is a fuller understanding of what the term *Client Engagement* means. Be prepared to be surprised.

As I review the research by the authors I've mentioned so far, one of the emerging themes is that most firms have little idea what their clients really feel about the service on offer. They have no measure, and therefore no evidence, of how deeply those clients are engaged. Moreover, the evidence is that most firms have little idea how to change that lack of Client Engagement.

What is interesting, and encouraging, is that this pivotal aspect of your business – Client Engagement – is not something that simply exists or not. Client Engagement is a conscious choice: it can be learned; it can be measured; it can be changed.

The following *Engage!* stage chapters will demonstrate the *why* and *how* of engagement in business. This you can do with new and existing clients, as well as with important centres of influence.

Join me as you prepare to engage more deeply with clients than you've ever imagined before.

Join me, as we examine examples of how others are reaping the rewards of fulfilment, meaning – and revenue – that flow from such engagement.

Chapter 7

Preparation: Attitude & Mindset

Before launching into your brave new world of more Ideal Clients, more fulfilling work, higher fees, more richness of life... you – the Hero of this story – need to be better prepared.

Here you learn to **Engage!** with your client community, and others, to design a more attractive Client Experience. A Journey, with you, that they will value, and talk about, for years to come.

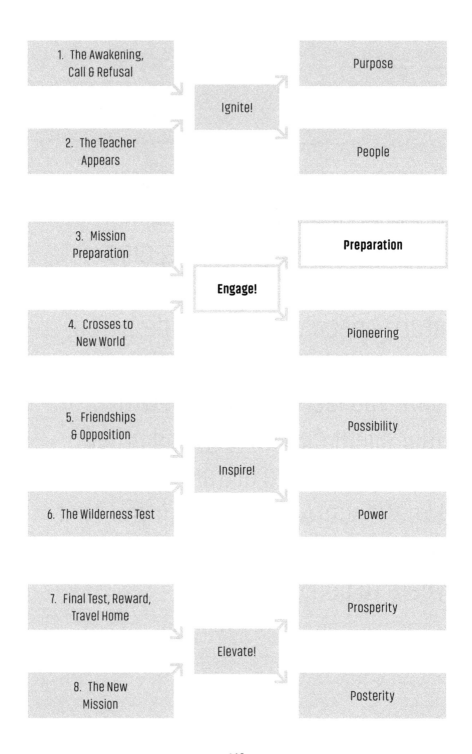

PREPARATION: ATTITUDE & MINDSET

Prioritise Preparation to Create Client Engagement

At the start of this book, you read Mary's story. It's a fascinating and inspiring one, isn't it?

Now it's time to share with you *how* Mary channelled her Passion and Purpose into disciplined business activity, which produced such astounding results.

Remember:

→   Mary had said that she couldn't sell to save her life (her words).
→   She had only recently qualified as a Chartered Financial Planner.
→   She had only 12 months' experience in this new profession.
→   Although successful in her previous profession as an accountant and Financial Director, she was struggling to gain clients in her new role.
→   She didn't understand how she could possibly command a minimum annual fee of more than £1,500 per annum. (Eventually, this figure would prove to be less than 20 percent of the value that clients place on her service today.)
→   She had presented me with a massive aspiration: to become the premier firm in the South East, working with women in the throes of a divorce. These divorcing women, she believed, were to be her Ideal Clients.

As the phrase goes, *"No pressure, then."*

How did we approach the task together?

What I'm going to do is answer that question by taking you through the initial steps she took. In other words, I'll show you what she did to **prepare** to access and *Engage!* the Right Clients.

> She was in danger of building a service based on flimsy knowledge and a bundle of assumptions.

Preparation Seeks Knowledge And Truth. Not Assumptions

This step, **Preparation,** asks you to go against the norm; you are going to be different to your peers.

You see, traditionally, a technically competent professional creates a service focusing on products and skills with which they are most familiar.

Nowadays they might call this service *"Our Value Proposition".*

They then take this proposition to the market, and use their character and personality, their skilled marketing and selling, to win new clients.

All perfectly normal stuff. Except *normal* is precisely what we're trying to get away from! Indeed, by now you'll appreciate that Mary was nothing like her *normal* peer group.

Becoming different calls upon two character qualities, identified by business philosopher Stephen R Covey as qualities of *primary greatness.*

They are:

1. Courage, and
2. Humility.

As I grew to understand Mary, it was obvious to me that she possessed both of these character qualities in abundance.

She had the courage to 'step into the dark' with me, to use skills and approaches she'd never encountered before.

She had the humility to admit her understanding of her intended Ideal Clients was limited. What little she did understand, she had gleaned from just a couple of client relationships with divorcing women.

Without a complete rethink, she was in danger of building a service based on flimsy knowledge and a bundle of assumptions.

She concluded that, if she was to build a service that would stand as a landmark in her profession, she had better build on something firmer than the shifting sands of guesswork.

What Mary needed were insights and views from more informed sources: including those within her Ideal Client community.

Mary Needed to Get Down to Some Serious Research

This research would be where her process of **Preparation** would start.

The question was: who was best qualified to help her in this research? Who should she interview first?

The three people who could help you

The way I see it, there are three groups of people who tend to be in a position to help us discover the truth about our Ideal Client community:

1. **Existing clients** already in the Ideal Client community.
2. **Potential clients,** again, already in the Ideal Client community.
3. **Centres of influence** already serving that community – for the sake of our narrative, let's call them *Gatekeepers.*

Now, my own experience is that each of these groups requires a different research interview approach. However, Mary's decision was to opt for Gatekeepers as the first subjects of her research, so, for now we'll focus on this group.

First, we identified the Gatekeepers to her Ideal Clients

As their name suggests, Gatekeepers are usually the most efficient gateway to your market. They already influence many people within your Ideal Client community – perhaps hundreds of people.

Of course, this route to your targeted community assumes that the Gatekeepers approve of you; it assumes they want to let you into the community they serve and influence.

In Mary's case, she decided that the most prominent Gatekeepers would be divorce lawyers. That made sense to me, and we focused our attention on them.

Mary had spoken to one or two lawyers, but I estimated that she needed to see at least 10. Fewer than that and she'd have little chance of learning what she needed to know to break into this world of Potential Clients.

"I believe in innovation, and that the way you get innovation is you fund research and you learn the basic facts."
Bill Gates

Approach This With Attitude

Second, we constructed the mental, emotional and verbal approach to the Gatekeepers

Mary was going to approach – completely cold – a profession that is reputed to be highly protective of client relationships. What's more, all she had heard told her that they had little regard for financial advisers in general.

We decided this research, this **Preparation,** required revealing, face-to-face conversations to gain credibility and trust.

But this wasn't going to be easy.
To even gain a meeting, Mary had to **Prepare** for her conversations in an unusual way.

→   She needed to do her homework: checking divorce lawyers' websites; requesting literature; finding the appropriate partner to approach.

→   She needed to remove all thoughts of selling and overt persuasion. She was undertaking *research,* not promoting her *value proposition.*

→   The purpose of the research would be to help her design – with their input – services that the Gatekeepers wished they possessed, and knew her Ideal Clients needed.

→   She appreciated that her first responsibility was to treat the Gatekeepers as if they were future clients. Their interests and opinions – not hers – needed to be at the centre of the discussion and research.

→ She needed to approach them with the desire to find out how she could best serve *them* first.

Our discussions helped her understand this principle:

→ A Gatekeeper is not merely someone you're trying to impress, with the sole objective of persuading them to send their clients to you – that's too self-focused an approach.
→ Instead, the Gatekeeper should be viewed as your 'Level 1' client. Your intention is to discover how you can first serve *the Gatekeeper;* and then to discover ways in which you can help *them* serve *their clients.*
→ It's this unusual, two-layered, service-focused paradigm that breaks down barriers and speeds the process of trust. It changes the nature of the relationship from *"What can you give me?"* to one of *"How can I help you to win in your business objectives and relationships?"*

Mary also needed to reset the expectations of these Gatekeepers:

→ She wasn't there to beg for crumbs from their table.
→ She was seeking to collaborate only with the best in their profession.
→ She was looking for opportunities to improve the reputation – and the flow of clients – for both parties... if she could.

What kept her spirits buoyant in all of this **Preparation** was her expectation that lawyers, naturally, would like to be asked for their counsel and opinion.

A Gatekeeper is not merely someone you're trying to impress, with the sole objective of persuading them to send their clients to you. That's too self-focused an approach.

As you can imagine, this shift of perspective and mindset was at odds with what Mary had been taught when she entered her new profession.

But, *being at odds* was precisely the spark that fired Mary's confidence and enthusiasm.

If there's one attitude that Mary exuded from the beginning of our coaching relationship, it was: *"Whatever's the norm in this industry today, I aim to take a completely different approach and test it out!"*

Ever the maverick. Ever the **Pioneer**. Ever the model of courageous action.

We constructed a simple phone conversation to create initial meetings with her Gatekeepers.

Then we constructed a series of questions (that I'll share with you in the next chapter, *Preparation: The Right Questions*). These would help her understand what those lawyers would really, really like from her. All she would need to do was decide:

→ Whether it was possible for her to create such a service.

→ Whether creating such a service was in line with her Passionate Purpose, her Heartfelt Values and her Unique Abilities.

"Research is to see what everybody else has seen, and to think what nobody else has thought."

Albert Szent-Györgyi

Let's Summarise What Mary Had Learned So Far

Remember, this whole chapter is about *Preparation.* This means:

→ **Preparing** yourself to meet those Gatekeepers and Ideal Clients who can help you see the world the way that they do.

→ **Preparing** yourself by setting aside your assumptions about what Value looks like.

→ **Preparing** yourself to be taught, before trying to teach.

→ **Preparing** your homework before conducting a research conversation.

→ **Preparing** the expectations of the Gatekeepers, so that you're seeking opportunities to help each other serve clients in a mutually-beneficial way.

"A moment's insight is sometimes worth a life's experience."

Oliver Wendell Holmes Jr

Ask Better Questions

What Mary intended to achieve with her research was to create a partnership with (in this case) the Gatekeepers of her Ideal Clients. My experience shows that such a partnership of minds and hearts results in a service more valuable than either party is likely to have imagined.

As I'll explain more fully in the next chapter, the questions you'll employ in your own research are likely to be different in their detail, depending on which community you approach:

1.   Existing clients, or
2.   Potential clients, or
3.   Gatekeepers to both

However, the intent of those questions will be the same: that is, to go beyond what might seem obvious, or assumed, and – together – seek what might be possible... if only someone would ask.

It's a radical thought: the adviser seeking to be advised.
Of course, the person you're interviewing might not know what service options are available from your industry or your firm.

So, they're unlikely to immediately point out how you could serve them better.

But that's *our* responsibility: to design, and ask, the kind of questions that will illuminate and clarify what choices we could make possible.

In this situation, don't expect your research interviewee to do all your thinking for you; it's useful to already have a written range of possibilities for them to consider.

It's also your responsibility to listen and look for what others might want, but which they assume is not possible. We seek to innovate. Often, what emerges from research is something that surprises both parties.

So, in co-creating a valuable service, two capabilities emerge as being important:

1.   Skilled questioning
2.   Innovative thinking

As you now examine, learn and start to embrace those capabilities... You'll be developing the mental muscle power to launch your flight into a new world.

The Thinking Bench

I've previously mentioned the Summer of 2012, the London Olympics. Our family still recalls, and speaks of, the joy we felt throughout those days.

At the time, Wendy could barely walk 20 steps without stopping for breath.

This was before her heart operation. (Today, she comfortably swims 20 lengths.) So, we pushed her around the London Stadium in a wheelchair, and then allowed for half an hour to climb the steps to our seats.

But the scenes we witnessed still bring smiles to our faces and wonder to our hearts.

Yes, we rejoiced in seeing the might of athletes like Ennis and Farah, Hoy and Trott, Wiggins, Ainslie and Dujardin, Rutherford and Stanning. And who could forget the mighty Usain Bolt?

But the Paralympic athletes made us gasp in awe.

Beefy, grizzly men on either side of us bawled like babies at the sight of the David Weirs and the Hannah Cockrofts with seemingly jet-propelled wheelchairs.

Our spirits were lifted, not just by their vanquishing their competitors and claiming gold, but also by their overcoming *"Am I Less than?"* to become *"Greater Than We Thought Possible!"*

Competition demands the best of us.
But I wonder, when this spills over into our working life, whether we know when to stop vanquishing, dominating, coercing.

I see messages that encourage us to be powerful, fierce and self-glorifying.
We continue to separate, divide, go our own way. We become *them* and *us*.

I remember watching a 60-second video that reminded me that what I really need – in my personal and business life – is to work together with others. To look for opportunities to improve another's life. To be more generous.

After watching that, I thought back to the many people – leaders and followers in business – whom I have coached, pro bono, for an hour, or two or three, during the last 15 years.

Their gratitude has always been effusive.
I feel like laughing with the memory and the enjoyment of it all.

As I coached them, I knew that most would never become clients. But surely, I can afford one hour to help someone who feels lost, confused, can't I?

When I behave like that, when I collaborate with another, to see what we can create together to lift and serve them... it washes back and flows over me.

I feel more at peace.
I feel more whole.

To find opportunities to be more generous and collaborative, and less desperate for our share, or our need to be right.

To be one.

Doesn't this make of our world a more delightful, more abundantly rich and surprisingly peaceful place?

What Have You Learned?

→   What is your experience in working with centres of influence, or Gatekeepers, to create a steady flow of referrals?

→   Most successful professionals (solicitors, accountants) tend to be specialists, not generalists. Which specific types of clients do your Gatekeepers work with?

→   In these relationships, have you educated them regarding a specific type (niche) of Ideal Client which you're happy to work with? Or do you find yourself feeling obligated to accept whatever they send to you?

→   Do you try to sell the benefits of your services when you meet with Centres of Influence and Gatekeepers? Or have you developed a structure of questioning that allows you to discover ways to help them first?

What Will You Do Now?

→   Which of the steps in this chapter will you test first?

→   What steps will you take to identify those Centres of Influence who specialise in a particular type of market?

→   What could you offer, show, or provide to these Centres of Influence (apart from money, which is the start of a tacky relationship) that will make them sit up and listen to the **Possibility** of creating a better service?

→   What **Preparation** will you do before approaching the next Centre of Influence?

Chapter **8**

Preparation: The Right Questions

Do What Others Daren't Do

Let's rejoin Mary as she embarks upon arranging her first meetings.

Remember, she had chosen the route of approaching Gatekeepers to her Ideal Client community. This was to prove an inspired decision.

I'd set her the task of arranging 10 meetings in 12 weeks. I didn't know of any other adviser who had met this many lawyers or solicitors in such a short time. So, I was staggered when she announced that she'd met *13* legal practices in fewer than eight weeks!

Trusting in her research approach, and not succumbing to the temptation to slip into selling or persuasion mode, Mary had engaged in conversations that proved unusually revealing.

The feedback from lawyers led Mary to conclude that their acceptance, trust and input came not because of what she'd *said,* but because of what she'd *asked.*

As anticipated, the (mostly female) lawyers made it clear that they loved being asked for their opinion.

Because of her new-found style of *asking better questions,* she found that lawyers also discussed their clients' behaviour patterns in helpful detail.

She discovered that, all too often, divorcing women had allowed their husbands to take control over their finances. Now, facing divorce, they were left with little information or insight into their future financial welfare. They felt confused and out of control.

Another oft-repeated comment was that these clients weren't in the mood to be patronised by another male. So, Mary, being a Mary, not a Mark, suited the lawyers perfectly.

Add to that her ability to listen carefully, and ask *sensitive questions* without a self-interested agenda, and hers was a winning formula.

That's not to say that Mary didn't pose "What if?" questions to suggest approaches and tools she felt many lawyers had never used. But she intuitively knew how to allow the lawyers to lead the conversations – once she'd asked the right questions.

Mary came to realise that this supposedly 'soft' information was far more valuable to her than any commercial logic or metrics.

She didn't need to be a therapist.

But what she did need was to create a service laden with relevant value, which – when articulated online, offline, verbally or in writing – clearly showed that she *understood*.

"Whoever understands the customer best, wins."
Lou Rossi

Skilled Questioning: Here's How

So, **what on earth *do* you ask** to help a Gatekeeper become a partner with you? How do you get them to help create a service they'd love, if only someone would design it?

In particular, what did Mary ask to create such astonishing results?

Well, below are some specific questions that Mary and others have found effective in helping you better understand the world of your Gatekeeper(s).

> The feedback from lawyers told her that their acceptance, trust and input came not because of what she'd **said**, but because of what she'd **asked.**

Remember, in all of the questions I'm going to share with you, the language and style need to be your own. All I'm doing is suggesting the nature and structure of questions:

→ **Firstly, I recommend you ask the Gatekeeper to clarify their areas of specialisation, expertise and niches.**
Of course, if you've defined your Ideal Client niche properly, this will, in large measure, already be answered for you. However, I find that a wonderful way of starting the conversation is to focus on them, like this:

"I'm curious... Why this specialisation for you? And how did this come about?"

→ **You'll ask the Gatekeeper about the characteristics and demographics of Ideal Clients in their niche.**

For example:

"Firstly, can you help me understand the demographics of your Ideal Client? By that, I mean, what age group, income levels, location, and so forth, best identifies your Ideal Client?"

→ **Why would clients prefer to work with their law firm, rather than their competitors'?**

You might ask:

"What is it about your firm that attracts this kind of client to you... rather than to your competitors?"

→ **What are their plans for the increased success of their firm?**

That might be couched in this way:

"From what little I understand, you've enjoyed success in your specialised field. What's the intention now, as you look to the future? How do you maintain and improve on that success, given competition and other market forces?"

→ **What are the biggest challenges they experience in serving their niche market?**

That question might sound like this:

"I find that each type of client I've served presents their own unique demands and challenges. I wonder... what are the most challenging aspects of working with your particular type of client?"

→ **What would make their lives easier as they strive to serve their clients?**

That question might sound like this:

"As you look back on your work with clients... what information do you wish you had known earlier? And how would that have helped you?"

→ **What is their experience of working with financial advisers or planners?**

That question might sound like this:

"Although I have only limited knowledge, I understand that the experience solicitors have in working with my profession is a real mixed bag. I'd love to hear your experience of previously working with financial planners. For example, how, as a profession, we could have served you better."

→ **Then there is this question, which can lead to all sorts of illuminating conversations. But don't be surprised if you are initially met with a blank stare:**

"Imagine you were me – a financial planner – and there was no limitation on your skills and resources. How would you best help and serve this firm of lawyers – your firm?"

Whatever you do, don't be tempted to jump into your finest sales pitch here!

If they respond by saying something like, *"Well, I don't know... How could you help this firm?"* Hold to your brief. You're here to do research, and to incorporate their views.

So, to that question, you might respond like this:

"Great question! And that's the purpose of my research. What I'd like to do is digest all that you've told me... factor in other views from my wider research... and come back to you with some service ideas to answer that. Would you be open to critiquing what I've created, once I've redesigned our services?"

Few clever presentations can match the results achieved by those who go armed with the desire to discover and understand, rather than to persuade.

Leave The Door Wide Open

Whoever is the subject of your research interviews, the **Power** of well-designed questions in opening doors to people's hearts and minds has to be witnessed to be believed.

As with any new skill, practise (and practise and practise). This is an essential part of your Journey.

Moreover, the intent of your questions needs to be focused on serving, not on selfishness. You'll find that most people are incredibly insightful in such conversations. Selfish intent will surface quickly – even if the other person can't quite put their finger on why.

Yet, even in your earliest attempts at crafting, practising and courageously using these incisive questions, I promise you some wonderful surprises.

Those who have invested in this approach have found that credibility and trust develop far faster in an environment of asking and listening. Few clever presentations can ever match the results achieved by those who go armed with the desire to discover and understand, rather than to persuade and coerce.

In the next chapter, on *Pioneering,* we'll examine what you're going to do with all of this new information, knowledge and insight. Because the question is:

→   How do you convert this new-found knowledge into action that creates better relationships?
→   And how do you convert this into action that serves and changes lives?

Having said that, the last thing you want to do is spend weeks and months designing an amazing new service, only to find that your Gatekeepers have forgotten all about you.

So, you need to leave the door wide open for continued conversations.

In your position, I have tended to say something like this:

"Thank you so much for the time you've set aside today. I don't regard your generosity lightly. I'm going to spend the next few weeks considering what I could create in the light of all that you've said to me today.

My intention is two-fold:

1. *To create a valuable service for the client community we both wish to serve.*
2. *To integrate those ideas and tools that might help you enhance the service you provide to those clients.*

Once I've designed this new service, I'd like to show you what that looks like. More importantly, I'd like you to critique it, telling me whether I've listened properly and understood you well.

There's a great deal to do here, both offline and online. But I sincerely believe that my effort will be worth it.

So, could we review the fruits of this labour in, say, six to eight weeks?"

Conclude With This Door-Opening Question

It's now time to remind the Gatekeeper that you're in research mode.

Importantly, you need to help them understand that your research requires a solid base of data. Therefore, there's a good deal of research you've yet to fulfil. Once you've done that research you'll be in a stronger position to design a service that has substance and is backed by a fair amount of evidence.

When it's clear that they appreciate this, I encourage you to conclude with the question that can open door after door for you – doors which, without their help, might remain closed.

You ask them this:

"If you were me... who would you meet with next, to continue your research?"

I'd like to point out that even this question requires good **Preparation:**

→ Ideally, you should already have identified the names of, say, 10 people who look as if they might be potential Gatekeepers (social media services like LinkedIn are useful here).
→ Then, ask your interviewee if they know any of the potential Gatekeepers.
→ Ask for an introduction to anyone they might know, no matter how casual that acquaintance.
→ Otherwise... ask permission to use the Gatekeeper's name when calling the next person.

You need to show that you're serious about the relevance of the next person you see. Make it clear that this research process is something you're going to conduct thoroughly.

The concluding question above is where your courage will be tested. So, let me give you a little encouragement.

It's not unusual for clients I've coached to expand their circle of contacts and introductions in this way.

Indeed, I remember well working with a client in Northern Ireland who started with three Gatekeeper research meetings: he eventually found himself in front of 18 of their peers!

The Power of well-designed questions in opening doors to people's hearts and minds has to be witnessed to be believed.

What About Research Interviews With Existing or Potential Clients?

It won't have escaped your notice that I've spent most of this chapter on Preparation focusing on how to work with Gatekeepers.

But what about similar interviews with existing (or even potential) clients?
Does that require a different approach?

Well, yes it does.

So, let me point to two approaches that work well during the early part of a research interview with either group.

As before, I wish that I'd innovated both approaches. But I can't claim that honour. Sadly, I can't recall where I first came across each approach. But I wouldn't mind wagering that they emerged whilst studying the reports, books and podcasts created by Julie Littlechild and Steve Wershing, CFP®.

First, we'll look at 'Their Greatest Client Experience'

This approach is well designed for the early part of a research interview.

What you're aiming to do is to:

→   Understand where and why the person you're interviewing had a Great Client Experience.
→   Use that experience as a benchmark to help your firm rise to that 'Great' level.

What's important is that you remove yourself from the centre of this discussion and look at what's happening in the wider world.

There are thousands of organisations around us from whom we can learn a great deal. Organisations that provide eyebrow-raising levels of brilliant service, astonishing everybody who engages with them.

Almost certainly, the person you're interviewing has had such an experience.
You need to understand how this person feels about those organisations – and why.

This approach requires setting aside our egos... and discovering how we too can become memorable in the minds and hearts of our clients.

With that in mind, and imagining that you're with an existing client, here's how the conversation could progress:

"I'm curious... setting aside our relationship for the moment, and considering the world at large... what is the single greatest service experience you've ever had?"

Once they've explained that experience... it's time to go deeper. To do that, you could use questions such as these:

→   *"Hmmm, I wonder why that particular experience came to mind?"*
→   *"How did that experience make you feel?"*
→   *"How did you first hear about that organisation?"*
→   *"Can you recall what happened when you first contacted them?"*
→   *"Can you recall any key moments, where they captured your attention whilst delivering their service?"*
→   *"Is there anything memorable about what happened afterwards; how they served you on an ongoing basis?"*
→   *"What words would you now use to describe this organisation?"*

Now, you don't need to pepper them with all of these questions (although some clients might thoroughly enjoy going into this detail). Nevertheless, with this new knowledge, you're better informed to understand the kinds of actions or communication that organisations undertake to become memorable to your client.

After a research interview like this, the question you'll be asking is obvious:

"How do we create these feelings and memorable moments for our (existing and future) clients?"

Second, we'll look at an approach that's perfect for existing clients

To help you structure this part of the conversation effectively, we'll be looking at a framework called *Come, Stay, Leave.*

The conversation might sound like this:

"I'd like to ask a question that is not easy for me. You'll see why when I ask it.

What I'd like to understand is how you view our relationship. And that means asking you three simple questions. Those questions are called Come, Stay and Leave."

You'll see what I mean in just a moment.

The First Question: COME
"What caused you to COME to our firm in the first place?

By that I mean: why did you choose to work with us, from all of the alternatives you had available?
What was the trigger that caused you to seek out our advice?"

The Second Question: STAY
"What are we doing that makes you comfortable to STAY working with our firm?

For example, if someone asked you to describe how we had helped you, what would you say?"

If they respond with something like, *"You've looked after us,"* then respond:

"That's interesting. I'm pleased that you feel we have. But, I wonder, what does that mean exactly?
*In what **particular ways** do you feel we've 'looked after' you?"*

Then get the client to try articulating the outcomes – the changes or the results – of your work together. Learn to get behind glib answers!

The Third Question: LEAVE
"Thank you for that feedback."

Now for the third part of the question – the feedback that most of us in business try to avoid.

"What might we do (or not do) that would cause you to become dissatisfied... and LEAVE to find another adviser to work with?"

Whatever they respond, never, ever become defensive! As my wife, Wendy, says when dealing with our children, *"Soak it up. Learn from it."*

I'll go further: *be grateful* that the client trusts you enough to speak both honestly and openly with you.

*"Thank you. This is such **helpful feedback** from you. And I'm grateful!"*

In today's marketplace, your knowledge is either current and relevant, or you're on the way out.

"Did you hear that, Aunt Sheila?

Did you hear it, in the night? I swear I could hear someone shuffling around outside the house."

She chuckled, answering: *"Honey, that's just the hermit crabs dragging their shells around in the cool of the night time. Remember, we're just a few yards from the beach as far as they're concerned."*

I have to be honest, for the first two nights it had scared me.

These houses were vulnerable to intruders of any sort. Everything seemed to be left open on this part of Grand Cayman.

I was a naïve 28-year old, albeit full of my own intelligence. Visiting these relatives, a turbo prop flight from Jamaica, was an unforgettable holiday. I met aunts and uncles who seemed to me wise, well-educated, successful.

One aunt mentioned to me that she was thinking of taking another degree, to help improve her opportunity of gaining a better teaching position. I can't recall exactly how old she was. But certainly, to a rather self-absorbed 28-year-old, even mid-40s looked pretty ancient.

My response to her passing comment was, *"But, Auntie... you'll be, let's say, 48 years old by the time you get that degree!"*

With a withering look and pitying smile, she responded:
"Young David. I'll be 48 years old anyway. Why not be 48 years old with a degree in a sought-after subject?"

That shut me up.

Experiences like that have led to my understanding of the **Power** of lifelong learning – a principle and practice made more necessary by the pace of change that all businesses are grappling with today.

In today's marketplace, your knowledge is either current and relevant, or you're on the way out.

With this perspective, worrying about the investment of time into a new Journey is somewhat myopic.

Rather than worry about the passage of time, why not concern yourself with the **measurably different impact** your actions will have on your firm, your revenue, your clients... and everybody else engaged with the person you're becoming?

The underlying question is: does all of this research and partnering with existing clients, potential clients and Gatekeepers really make a measurable difference to your firm, to your revenue?

I believe you already know the answer to that.

I also believe that the future of this next generation of financial planners will include much closer partnering with clients and Gatekeepers.

I recognise that it's a radical shift in thinking and behaviour. I also recognise that it involves an investment of time, energy and education that you currently don't undertake.

Yet, look at the results you've already observed, just by reading this far!

Having said that, it would be unfair of me not to let you appreciate the reality of what's needed, if you're going to achieve the kinds of results you've now read about:

→   Mary spent two months interviewing sufficient Gatekeepers to provide enough data to work with.
→   She then devoted three months to redesigning her services.
→   Then she spent three months getting back to all the divorce lawyers who had helped in her research.

Now, you might say, *"What? That's at least eight months before I'm likely to get any return on my investment!"*

Well maybe. Maybe not. Maybe you can work more quickly than that.

Embarking on The Soul Millionaire Journey might take you time; you'll be months older when the measurable rewards start flowing in.

But, the fact is, you'll be months older anyway!

Why not reach that point in your life with the **Power** to completely change your direction and your destination?

Why not learn from the masters of the skies?

They Prepare for mighty journeys by investing time in building mighty strength first.

What Have You Learned?

→ When was the last time you conducted face-to-face research interviews with your existing clients?

→ Who designed that research exercise: you, or a skilled, professional researcher or marketing consultant?

→ If you've conducted these exercises yourself in the past... were you aware of how to test genuine Client Engagement?

→ How carefully have you studied the differences between client loyalty, client satisfaction and Client Engagement?

→ What measurable commercial factors do you believe define whether a client is truly engaged – or not?

What Will You Do Now?

→ Since Client Engagement creates such enormous differences in the financial, emotional and cultural impact on a business... when do you plan to learn more about what Client Engagement really means?

→ Who will you turn to for guidance in your research? And when?

→ Which existing clients can you identify, who might have knowledge (or influence) in the Ideal Client market you'd like to target?

→ How many of these conversations could you arrange in the next three to six months?

Chapter 9

Pioneering: Through Your Positioning

This is where your adventure takes
a leap forward; where you leave
the borders of the familiar, the safe,
the normal.

This is where you start to Soar,
carving your own, unique path
based on all you've discovered.

Now you start to lead, not follow.
You'll become not just **better than.**
You'll be **the only one who...**

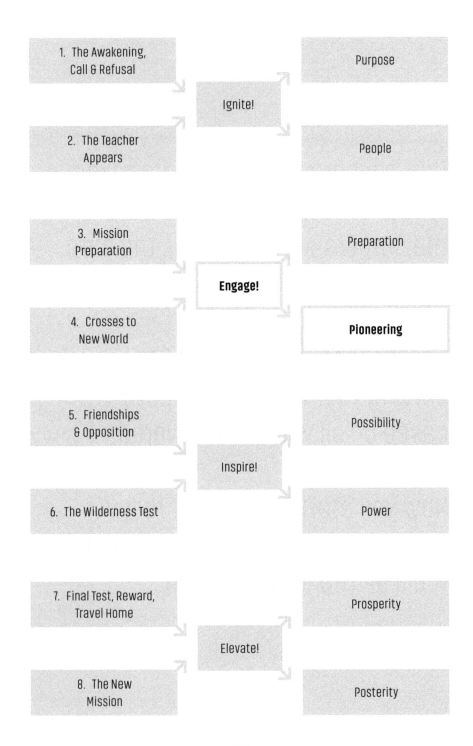

Why Be a Pioneer?

The term Pioneering has a romance attached to it.
There's a spirit that's conjured up, images that are invoked.

By their nature, **Pioneers** take greater risks, cast aside homely comforts and step into the dark without necessarily seeing a light at the other end.

Pioneers embrace the belief that, somewhere across this wilderness of uncertainty, lies a land that will make their hearts sing.

Pioneers tend to make others uneasy. They attract attention – often against their will. They attract criticism. They threaten what's accepted, what has always been done around here.

Yet it is the Pioneers' questioning of:

→   *"What's out there?*
→   *What's possible?*
→   *Why not?"*

... that leads to answers and outcomes; to solutions to problems. And they take our breath away.

Since *you* are the Hero of this Journey, this is where you take the mantle of **Pioneer**. Right now is when you're ready to do what others dare not do, creating services, relationships and impacts that others only talk about.

You'll be engaging the **Spirit of Pioneering** to guide you through the next three steps on your Journey. These steps naturally follow the Preparation you've invested in.

You might recall that the three **Pioneering** steps we'll be examining are:

i.   **Positioning**
ii. **Product**
iii. **Pricing.**

By 'Positioning'... we mean the messages communicated by what you do, say or write to your Ideal Client market.

By 'Product'... we mean the magnetic, relevant, make-a-difference service you'll create, once you've done your homework about what your Ideal Client market really, really wants.

By 'Pricing'... we mean charging fees that reflect the wisdom, knowledge, skills, time and energy you're bringing into play, to serve your client. But, far more importantly, fees that reflect how much your clients value your extraordinary and relevant service in their lives.

Pioneers use the little-known principles of client engagement

You'll not be surprised when I say that **Pioneering** also means learning how to help existing and potential clients become more deeply-engaged with you and your firm.

After all, **Preparation** and **Pioneering** are the two main components of this *Engage!* stage of your Soul Millionaire Journey.

These principles of deeper engagement are also woven into all elements of the *Inspire!* Stage. But it is here, as you start Pioneering, that you'll learn what those principles look like. This understanding will guide your steps and your thinking as you progress.

Let's Pioneer How to Become More Relevant to Your Market

I've previously described how I was given my first lesson in marketing by a successful young entrepreneur, Doug Woodward.

With his encouragement I focused my attention on a specific type of client: software consultants. Since Doug and I had each spent eight years of our careers in the IT recruitment sector, this was a world we knew well.

I took a risk and travelled up and down the country meeting with the Gatekeepers of my Ideal Client community. In this case my research was with hard-nosed managing directors of national recruitment agencies.

Their input proved to be invaluable.

What they *didn't* want was to help me sell insurance and pensions.

What they *did* want was for me to help their sales consultants close deals.

You see, their revenue came largely from persuading permanent employees to accept lucrative freelance or 'contract' assignments.

The one sticky moment for a recruitment sales consultant was getting the wannabe 'contractor' to put pen to paper and sign the first contract.

The legislation at the time required each contractor to:

→   Set up their own limited liability company, obviously with a unique company name.
→   Appoint a company secretary.
→   Organise their own bookkeeper, accountant and tax affairs.

Ah! Now I knew what the problem was!
Now I knew what all parties *really* wanted.

My instincts told me that if I could design and create a speedy solution – a solution where I was the first person the new 'contractor' would call – it wouldn't be difficult to get them to meet me.

My instincts were right.

I spent the next three months finding all the companies who could provide those first-steps services (a limited company, an accountant, a company secretary) that contractors needed before signing on the dotted line.

All the sales consultant had to do was to give my beautifully designed brochure to the potential contractor. Then the two of them would phone my office.

And within five minutes both parties had enough information to sign the contract.

Bingo!

"Differentiation is one of the most important strategic and tactical activities in which companies must engage. It is not discretionary."
Theodore Levitt

Stop Competing, Start Pioneering

My brochure directed the new contractor to me, so that they could be introduced to their bookkeeper and accountant.

Within a week, they were eager to meet the person who had expedited their entry into this new world (little ol' me).

At which stage they were ready to talk about replacing all the elements of their remuneration package that had disappeared when they changed from permanent employment, i.e.:

THE FLIGHT OF THE SOUL MILLIONAIRE

→ Their sickness and life insurances.

→ Their pensions.

→ Whatever else they wanted to organise with their new-found income.

Within months, I knew that I'd created something unique.
Here was a clearly articulated, structured service that the market really wanted. Here was something I had created in partnership with Gatekeepers.

There was only one other firm in the UK doing anything vaguely like this.
I wasn't competing. I was alone. Out on a limb. Heading through the wilderness.

I wasn't *better than*. I was the *only one who...*
This wasn't just different; this was dramatically different.

I was a *Pioneer!*

Six months later I left my cold, lonely attic office in King's Cross.

In another six months, we were receiving at least two referrals every single week. Every week!

My working life had changed forever.

Look Back And Connect The Dots

Time and again in my life, I've looked back to realise that I had been weaving a beautiful pattern with each courageous, small step in my work and my life.

In those moments I can see how random 'dots' of decisions and actions have combined to create something meaningful and, at times, life-changing.

I compare this process to the stunning works created by post-impressionist artists like Georges Seurat and Paul Signac.

Close up, their pictures present a random mass of coloured dots. But stand back... and the most hauntingly beautiful pictures unfold to our astonished eyes.

At the point in my career I've just described, I had no idea that I was learning the principles of **Positioning, Product** and **Pricing.**

Nor did I understand how all three subjects could help to increase Client Engagement in any business.

But now I can see that is precisely what I was doing.

In **Pioneering,** I want to reveal how *you* can set yourself apart from your peers in all of these areas.

In doing so, you'll also learn how to create a more deeply engaged client community: **a community that will help your firm create a steady flow of Ideal Clients.**

This is How You Start to Position Yourself

Working with Gatekeepers – in this case, IT recruitment agencies – I had blundered into my first lesson on **Positioning** a service or **Product.**

In simple terms, I had learned to 'own' a particular **Position** in the hearts and minds of two communities:

1.   My Ideal Clients
2.   The Gatekeepers to that Ideal Client community

I did this by creating the right messages, the right communication, to that Ideal Client community.

When either party thought of taking a particular course of action... my firm's name, my brand, my messages, were amongst those influences that arose in many of their minds.

The feedback, from both contractors and agencies, taught me that our firm was on their radar the moment the right circumstances arose in their work.

That's the Power of Positioning.

And the messages I had created in the process, and which stood out in my brochures, became part of the process of successful Client Engagement.

So, now we've created a three-part formula:

→   The Right Clients
→   The Right Questions
→   The Right Messages

Meanwhile, being Wildly Different in my **Positioning** also taught me the excitement and risks inherent in **Pioneering.**

Not everybody praised what I was doing.
Colleagues and acquaintances told me that I was spending time doing things that had nothing to do with investment, pensions and insurances.

They were right.

I was told that my success would depend upon grabbing the phone and putting myself in face-to-face sales situations. Writing nice brochures wasn't what being a financial adviser was all about.

Of course, to a large extent, they were right again.

Yet these very criticisms fired my determination to show them how hard-wired their thinking had become. The fact is, **Pioneers** will always be criticised.

During this process of Positioning, I made many costly, naïve mistakes.

But Pioneering definitely wasn't one of them.

Look at Other Positioning Pioneers

In the client stories I've shared so far, the **Positioning Pioneers** stand out.

Let's take Matthew (he of the deadly nut experience).

He has designed one of his two brands to attract and serve dentists.

Now, you might think that there's nothing special about that. But Matthew is crystal clear about the age group, problems and desired outcomes of his Ideal Client community.

Following a period of careful research by Matthew, the phrase below arose – almost as a joke – as we were coaching and planning one day.

He said, *"The mindset of my Ideal Client is: I'm a dentist... get me outta here!"*

Matthew found that the pressures of NHS dentistry had increased so much that the older generation of dentists desperately want to get out of the profession.

Consequently, everything Matthew uses to communicate – seminars, tri-fold brochures, website – is not only technically excellent, but supremely emotionally relevant to the *I'm a dentist... get me outta here!* mentality.

The Right Messages to the Right Market.

Richard in Hampshire knew precisely whom he wanted to attract.

After some months of coaching and persuasion, Richard finally focused on business owner-managers whose attitude to life and business was much like his. They'd probably also be in their 50s and be leading successful Hampshire-based businesses.

But when he used phrases like...

→ *"Stop the world. I want to get off."*
→ *"You've been so busy with your work that your dreams have become buried along the way."*

... they knew that he fully understood their feelings.

In Hampshire's business community, he owned that message to his future clients.

"Our memory is highly selective... in a crowded category, your difference might not be enough unless it is a dramatic difference."

Jack Trout

Then there's Alfie.

After his South American mining experience, Alfie quickly bought into the concept of carefully **Positioning** a firm.

His career had developed in a team, which focused almost entirely on clients employed in the petrochemical industry.

But, through keeping their eyes open to possibilities... Alfie and his colleague Anna found a Gatekeeper who started introducing them to young IT entrepreneurs – the sort of entrepreneurs who, when they hit the jackpot, can sell their ideas and companies for millions of pounds.

With the sensitive coaching skills that Alfie and his colleagues had learned during recent years, Alfie has now created an approach and service to this niche market that would be hard to copy without those skills.

And there's another Richard, west of London.

Richard has designed an unusual **Position** for his work with his Top 20 clients. His intention is to integrate into his service something that he already enjoys doing.

He found that clients loved to join him on his walks in some of the world's most beautiful and breathtaking places.

Imagine taking a client to the Lake District for a planning and review discussion. Or how about to the mountains of Scotland? Or perhaps for a challenging bike ride? Or simply meeting a client for a morning or afternoon in the refreshing peace of the New Forest?

It's ridiculous, isn't it? I mean, what has all that to do with financial planning?

But that's the whole point:

→ **Pioneers** shun the herd mentality of any industry or profession.
→ **Pioneers** run a completely different race.
→ **Pioneers** want to create a different culture, based on a different **Purpose,** fuelled by a different ethos.

Pioneers consider what clients would absolutely, passionately, love in a service. Then, if it's something in line with their values, they go ahead and design it.

Infuse Your Positioning With This Unique Ingredient

You'll recall, in the chapter on *The Three Catalysts,* I shared the story of Chesley Burnett 'Sully' Sullenberger III.

We looked at the X factor that made Sully's flight experience unique: his saving of 155 lives.

I concluded that the X factor in a small business is *you:*

→   The unique Journey in life that only *you* have travelled.
→   The person *you've* become, as a result of that Journey.
→   The person *you're* intentionally becoming, as a result of your **Purpose,** your intentions and where you're heading.

We're not cyborgs nor robots. We bring our humanity to our work, whether we believe it, recognise it or even like it.

In each of the stories of financial planners I've already shared with you, the unique 'story' of the Hero had relevance to the Ideal Client community the Hero wished to serve.
Their approach to serving their clients was deeply influenced by the difficulties, challenges, disappointments and heartaches they'd personally experienced in life. These experiences tended to inform and influence how they saw their Passionate Purpose in life and business.

Who you are and what you've become is part of your uniqueness in business.

Let the world know about it!

They might decide they like what they hear; they might dislike it intensely. Either way, that's good.

Why would you want to spend time with people who are not attracted by who you really are?

So, consciously map out your story. Clarify your Passionate Purpose. Then weave that into your Positioning, which you broadcast to the world.

Do that, and you'll own a Position on people's intellectual and emotional radars that is uniquely yours.

Seven Questions: Use Them to Sense-Check Your Positioning

If you're wondering how you can tell whether your **Positioning** is effective (or not), the following seven questions should prove valuable.

For some of these questions, accreditation must go to Steve Moeller, and his book *Effort-Less Marketing for Financial Advisors*.

(Please note: the following questions don't just apply to something you say on your website or in your marketing material. And we're certainly not talking about creating intellectually tempting elevator pitches – or whatever the latest marketing guru tactic might be.)

This is not merely about statements you make. These questions are far more a reflection of the way you and your firm think, believe and behave. Ask yourself:

1. Does my **Positioning** set me apart as a **Pioneer?** Does it strongly differentiate me and my firm?
2. Does my **Positioning** assertively filter out those who are unlikely to be my Ideal Clients?
3. Does my **Positioning** include frequent communication about my Ideal Client community: their problems, their needs and their desired outcomes?
4. Does my **Positioning** relate to something already in my (potential) Ideal Client's mind?
5. Does my **Positioning** communicate the potential solution to a high priority problem for my Ideal Clients?
6. Does my **Positioning** include educating clients about what really matters in their engagement with me?
7. Does my **Positioning** create curiosity, and feel credible and compelling to my audience?

You might only manage a 'yes' to questions 1. and 2. Even then, believe me, you're well on your way to creating a strong **Position** in the psyche of your Ideal Client community and their Gatekeepers.

"Financial Advisers... you'll pay a high price for thinking that you don't have a brand, or that you don't need one. Those with strong, differentiated brands... charge higher prices, acquire greater market share."

Keith E Niedermeier

If You're Going to Pioneer, Don't Fall into This Trap

The French have an interesting saying, an epigram by Jean-Baptiste Alphonse Karr in 1849: *"Plus ça change, plus c'est la même chose."*

Translated literally it means, "The more it changes, the more it's the same thing."

This is what I notice about trends and fads in business – or life in general...
Language and soundbite-thinking catch on quickly... until what was unusual and interesting becomes common and hackneyed.

So it is within the financial planning community.

When I meet individually with leaders in the sector, I ask them what is different and outstanding about their firm. Where do they believe they're ahead of the curve... leading the thinking and behaviour... standing out from the crowd?

In response to that question they start telling me:

→   How much they care about clients.
→   How wonderful they are at explaining the complex in a simple way.
→   How skilled they are at listening.
→   How much their work is centred on their clients' goals and objectives, not just their money.

Not surprisingly, they express these differences with some passion. The problem becomes clear when I (and other coaches and consultants whose reports I've studied) review the patterns in the comments of the hundreds of financial planners I've interviewed individually, or perhaps when I meet with a group of financial planning firms in a workshop.

Ask the group to scribble down three things that make them different, and (you're ahead of me, aren't you?) lo and behold! The same phrases crop up again and again and again throughout the group.

Yes, the sector is evolving and changing. But, if the bulk of firms feel that they're different and better in exactly the same way, then...

Well, they're hardly different, are they?

What's more, if identical language is being used from website to website and from conversation to conversation with potential clients and Gatekeepers... obviously, there's no hope that even experienced consumers could tell the difference!

So, using that language, and expressing those same differences, becomes a zero-sum game.

If you're going to **Pioneer,** and you're going to do that within your...

→   **Positioning**
→   **Product**
→   **Pricing**

... then I urge you to give thought to the various components that we're examining here. **There's no quick fix to becoming a Pioneer, nor to being memorable or renowned.**

When Wendy jumped on the name for my first book, *The Soul Millionaire,* I thought she was being daft. It was merely something I was mumbling about, along with other possibilities.

I was even more cynical when she said that this would be a great name for our company. Indeed, a name for me too, for when I was being introduced as a speaker in conferences and seminars.

I told her she didn't understand the secular business world I lived in. I would be laughed at, using such a spiritually suggestive name.

"Well," she responded, *"they might forget **you**. They'll probably forget what you said. But they'll never forget that unusual name: in business, it will be how your life is spoken about."*

I hate it when she's right.
She's almost always right.

Very little of what we do and say in life is memorable to others.

Yet there are moments when we hear or read something that changes our own views, even our behaviour – and therefore, the direction of our life.

Long after they're gone, people's messages and ideas can hold a Position in our minds, which is indelible. We might point to their human flaws and weaknesses, but their words are memorable nonetheless.

Ideas like Martin Luther King's dream.

Or Winston Churchill's immortal sentiment: *"Never in the field of human conflict was so much owed by so many to so few."*

Or these words from John F Kennedy: *"We choose to go to the moon, and do other things, not because they are easy, but because they are hard."*

I wonder... what do people *think* about when they hear the name of your firm, your organisation?

What do they *feel* when they do say that name?

Or are you leaning heavily upon being a *nice guy* or *girl...* in order to be memorable?

When you are convinced about what you do which is different...

When what you do points to something other than merely making more money...

When you can articulate that difference, so that others can understand...

Then you have a chance of being memorable.

Then **Positioning** will become more than a concept.
It will be how your business and life is spoken about.

What Have You Learned?

→ Do you recognise the lessons from your own life story that make you different from your peers?

→ What elements of your life experience have you purposefully woven into your business strategy and culture?

→ How does that story influence the way you'd love to serve your clients?

→ When a client mentions your organisation's name, does it immediately conjure up words, pictures and meaning in the mind of the listener?

→ What do you understand by the term *brand*?

→ When your team tells stories about your firm, what do those stories say about you, your beliefs, and why you're so different and memorable?

What Will You Do Now?

→ Think about the story of your life. Now, what can you take from that story that you'd like to recount to every new client? And what impact do you wish it to have?

→ Look at five of the industry's top 100 websites. How are you significantly different from them?

→ Having read how similar all the 'We're Different' statements are in your industry... when are you going to review what you've written... what you're saying... what you're teaching your team?

Chapter 10

Pioneering: Through Your Product

A Closer Look at Product

Let's be clear. In the context of what we're discussing in this chapter, the term Product is not to be confused with *Products.*

This is not about marketing and selling financial instruments, investment strategies and funds, software tools and platforms – although all of those could be a part of your **Product.**

In business and marketing strategy, **Product** can refer to whatever simple or sophisticated service you're providing to your market.

Your **Product** could include the intellectual, emotional and spiritual experience and journey that you're creating for your client as they work with you.

I agree, the initial **Product** I created for IT Contractors might not be relevant to your market. It might not be easily replicated by you.

But the principles taught by my story aren't hard to discern, nor are they difficult to apply.

Back to Mary

To make it easier for you to relate to the process of creating a **Pioneering Product...** let's continue a little further with Mary's story.

Following her research, the question Mary had asked sounded like this: *"How do I convert this new knowledge, from research, into action that serves and lifts and changes lives?"*

The answer was simple really (although I didn't say, *"Easy"*):

*"You build your **Product,** aligned with what you've discovered during these searching conversations. Then you go back and show the prototype of what you've built."*

Twelve weeks elapsed before Mary had a new service mapped out, with supporting material, online and offline.

At first glance, were you to review her list of services, they might not have appeared much different to that offered by any other experienced financial planner.

However, looking a little deeper, you might have become aware of what didn't appear. Missing were the mindless lists that normally read like this: *"We provide services to deal with your insurance, pensions, investments, inheritance tax planning, long term care... blah, blah, blah..."*

Not inspiring.

What she was clear about were the elements of her service, including tools like cashflow planning, that would prove most valuable to her Gatekeepers.

Encouragingly, one or two lawyers suggested that Mary enter the legal conversation sooner rather than later – an unusual element of her **Product.**

What stood out from the research was not the need for a list-of-things-we-do-each-year. What the lawyers highlighted was the need for empathy, patience and hand-holding during sensitive and highly-charged conversations about money.

Mary was overjoyed. This was what she had suspected and hoped.

Having said all of that... what Mary did understand was that there needed to be a clear structure, or framework, to her service. She needed to succinctly articulate this framework in writing. For this, she sought the services of a good copywriter.

All of this, the concepts and language, became part of her **Product**, part of what became her brand.

When, as agreed, she returned to 10 of those divorce lawyers, their response was encouraging.

Yes, it was another few months before the first couple of Ideal Clients were introduced to her by these lawyers. But the suitability and quality of those clients were spot on.

During the following 12 months, the formal introductions from the lawyers became more frequent and more valuable. Mary became increasingly skilled at working with both Gatekeepers and Ideal Clients.

Today, the tables are turned: Mary receives requests from divorce lawyers to endorse testimonials about *them* and *their* services.

Within a short period of time, Mary's differentiation and reputation have placed her in an enviable position within a sought-after professional community.

Let's now look at Matthew's Product

Represented in Matthew's clever tri-fold marketing brochures are a number of business components he has astutely drawn together:

→ The **Product** strapline *Today Is the Day* responds directly to the dentists' plea expressed in his research interviews: *"Get me outta here!"*

→ The first internal page summarises his firm's planning expertise:
   ⇨ Financial planning
   ⇨ Life planning (in other words, professional coaching skills).

→ The second internal page neatly summarises his firm's technical expertise:
   ⇨ Estate planning
   ⇨ Retirement planning
   ⇨ Investment management.

→ The third internal page introduces the consultancy expertise provided by associates in his business network:
   ⇨ Business consultancy and coaching
   ⇨ Exit strategy consultancy.

In each of these three areas of expertise – planning, technical and consultancy – Matthew aspires to be more than *'Good at what we do'.* He and his associates constantly strive to become *'Experts in our field'.*

On the rear of the tri-fold, Matthew has created a diagram, which – with clarity and a light, jargon-free touch – allows the potential client to understand the journey that Matthew is about to take them on.

What's more important is that, on the rear of the tri-fold, Matthew makes room for his X factor.

He tells the story of *That Piece of Bread,* but he also directs the reader to his website, where he shows the link between his Awakening, his personal journey, and his passion for serving his Ideal Clients.

This last element alone is unusual in the financial planning community. Combined with the other elements of his **Product...** the element marks Matthew out as one of the community's **Pioneers.**

Matthew's **Product** framework recognises two aspects that are present in the most effective Pioneering Products:

1. The **Product** is designed to specifically serve the Ideal Client community.
2. The **Product** highlights the specialisation and greatest expertise the firm wishes to present to the market – typically just one or two specialisations, no more.

Matthew weaves these two aspects throughout every fibre of the business:

→ By designing systems and processes that support the three main areas of expertise of the **Product;**

→ By educating his team, so that they all understand the roles they're playing in communicating and delivering the **Product;**

→ By developing his own skills so that the client feels that their engagement with his team is an uplifting, life-influencing experience.

> Wealth Management is about the application of mathematics and collective behaviour to the subject of money.
>
> Financial planning is about the application of money and individual behaviour to the subject of **life!**

Use This as Your Pioneering Product Benchmark

It's tempting, when designing your **Product,** to be excited about aspects of service that your industry has traditionally praised.

But, by now you'll recognise that my intention is to constantly question tradition where tradition does not best serve the client.

There's too much of this

What most firms tend to concentrate on is the creation and delivery of what I term *output.*

Output is all the energy, time, skills and resources devoted to *"how much we deliver to you, our client"* (largely, to justify our fees), including:

→ How many review and planning meetings your firm holds with each client each year.
→ How many financial plans you create for each client.

Output (or volume of visible activity) is what I regularly see driving frenetic, furious and stressful activity within many firms, including:

→ How many investment reports you send to clients.
→ How many newsletters, blogs and podcasts you broadcast to keep in touch.

But – useful as it might seem – output misses the point completely.

A Pioneering Product looks more like this

Firstly, I'd suggest you review the chapter on People. There you can begin to see what's required of a brilliant **Product.**

I would argue that the measure of a brilliant **Product** is the *change* that it instigates. In The Soul Millionaire Journey, we have a special term for that kind of change. So, let's discuss that term now.

It's about Outcomes

The question, the benchmark, that every **Product** can be measured against, is this:

*"What are the **outcomes** created by the journey that the client experiences when engaging with you and your firm?*

Specifically, what are the outcomes:

→ *In your client's healthy relationship with money, and*
→ *In your client's life?"*

I believe that everything your **Product** does needs to be directed towards, and measured against, helping your clients to attain positive outcomes in those two areas. Everything.

I believe that is the purpose and measure of our work.

I believe that a firm's **Product** that *doesn't* take this into account shows a misunderstanding of the **Possibility** and **Power** of the firm's professional role.

The role is then reduced to the creation of solutions to money problems.

For me, there is a difference between services such as wealth management... and the professional role of financial planner.

Wealth management is, surely, about the application of mathematics and collective behaviour to the subject of *money.*

On the other hand...

Financial planning is about the application of money and individual behaviour to the subject of *life!*

Now, such a solution-based activity might require considerable knowledge, skill and hard work. You, and your team, might be handsomely paid for this activity.

But in the long term – compared to what could be happening – the impact on your clients' lives and your team's lives will lack the meaning and Purpose that could be theirs. And yours.

The Thinking Bench

I'd seen Matthew excited before. It's in his entrepreneurial nature. But this was something different.
He looked hypnotised as he spoke about it.

For long seconds, I lost him as his mind flew clear out of the window...
And returned, bringing his honeymoon memory back with it.

"I remember the moment I first looked over the Pacific Ocean from the Post Ranch Inn.

Thinking back to that moment, I can see that it changed me. Forever. We were on our honeymoon in the summer of 2013 and life could not have been better.

The Post Ranch Inn?
Well, it's a super high-end, luxury resort in the Big Sur region of California. Few know of its existence. But if you're musing through any of the luxury magazines, you're likely to spot it.

It appears on all sorts of Top 10 lists: Top 10 Views, Top 10 Infinity Pools, Top 10 Restaurants, and so on. Even today, I'd say it's my number one place to be on planet Earth.

Yet this has nothing to do with the luxurious accommodation, the mind-blowing food or the impeccable service.

It is more to do with the place itself, the setting. The magic of the California coast does something to me. Being in this place bathes me in a sense of inner calm. It's a feeling I experience nowhere else. And to me that feeling is priceless.

I can see you want to search for the pictures now. But, honestly, they don't do it justice. They can't.

Because, as I stared in dumbfounded awe over the calm, deep blue ocean, I knew this was somewhere I wanted to return to again, and again, and again.

There was just one tiny problem: The Post Ranch Inn costs over $2,000 per night!

On the day we left, I vowed that we would return regularly in the years that followed. I just hadn't quite figured out how we would pay for it.

I admit that, on that mind-shifting honeymoon of ours, we stayed in several places that were similar in terms of price and luxury. But none of them came close to the effect that the Post Ranch Inn had on me. On us.

Our visit here was a turning point in my life. I wanted to feel that feeling again and see that view again. And I certainly wasn't about to let money stop me!

If I were to try to sum up the impact on us, it would sound like this: 'It is like fairy dust has been sprinkled all over the place, and upon us, as we immersed ourselves in it. Fairy dust.'"

If you allow Matthew's words to rest upon you for a while, you'll realise that one person's imagination can create an experience – which was the Post Ranch's **Product** – that takes another person's breath away. Even change the way that *other person* looks at life.

If we exercised the courage, even our childhood games prove that we can create the extraordinary.

When it comes to designing your own **Product...** you can copy what everybody in your sector is doing. That's easy. Or you can turn your imagination to sprinkling clients with fairy dust.

That's more demanding.
And more gloriously rewarding.

What Have You Learned?

→ In what way does your **Product** reflect your commitment to serving a particular type of client, an Ideal Client?

→ Where did you first gain your ideas about developing your present client services, your **Product?** A best-practice meeting? A consultant? A colleague? Your former boss?

→ What message does your **Product** say about the main intent of your service? Is it to manage investments? To save tax? Create a coherent life/financial plan, letting that guide your advice?

→ What research has been invested in the design of your services? And by whom? You? Your team? Or a professional, skilled in the science of research?

→ How have you visually expressed the journey and experience your new clients will have when working with you?

→ How do you shape clients' expectations, so that they realise their client experience is delivered by your team, not just by you?

What Will You Do Now?

→ If money were no object, what kind of experience would you like to provide for your favourite clients?

→ What do you feel needs to be done now, so that the journey and experience that your clients undertake have the greatest impact on their lives?

→ How will you reshape your **Product,** so that wealth management and financial planning are not confused in your client's mind?

→ How will you discover what your clients really, really think about your **Product...** rather than what you *hope* they think?

Chapter 11

Pioneering: Through Your Pricing

Let's Prod The Hot Topic

As I read the weekly financial magazines (offline and online) aimed at the financial planning community, it's interesting to see how emotions are stirred by topical subjects. Considered, balanced commentary vies for space and attention with strident, angry, even defamatory voices.

It will always be so in public forums.

One of the perennial topics that flares up is the matter of how both these communities choose to be paid.

This subject of fees and commissions attracts polarised and passionate commentators. For example, those who even hint that the remuneration model is inappropriate or outdated are often openly attacked and vilified.

We shouldn't be surprised about this, considering that the subject pierces the heart, soul and wallet of any business.

By discussing the approach of Pioneering Pricing, my intention is not to proclaim one method of charging clients as more correct or ethical than another.

However... what I would like you to consider is *why* some highly paid, fulfilled, successful financial planners approach this subject with a vastly different perspective to their peers. Just as important, I ask you to consider what you think this different perspective might look like.

What thought processes have helped some firms identify a completely different way of charging for their services, when compared with the model of the previous 20 years?

Because, the fact is, some advisers have changed the rules about why and how clients value their services.

These firms are **Pioneers.** They've stepped back, looked at the traditional views on commissions and fees and they've found those views lacking cohesion and logic.

Moreover, they don't get involved in the general mêlée of discussion about fees. They don't, because they believe that the wrong subjects are being discussed.

Listen to This Comment From Andrew

I first met Andrew when his software firm acquired one of my corporate clients.

Andrew's company went on to orchestrate a reverse takeover of a quoted IT group. That company was in trouble, and the shares almost worthless. As the new Group Financial Director, Andrew helped resurrect the company, until it once more had credibility on the stock market.

By age 43, Andrew had fulfilled many of his financial goals by selling his now-valuable shares in the company. At around this time, he embraced Christianity – a change which noticeably altered his views on corporate leadership.

For the next few years, he enjoyed mentoring businesses that were struggling. This led to chairmanship of three European banks, as well as other leadership mentoring projects.

For a few years, I was fortunate to have Andrew as my mentor. I learned a great deal from both his commercial experience and his wisdom.

I share this story with you to indicate Andrew's success in both business and finance. Not only is he a knowledgeable investor, he also brings credibility and character to his work.

But listen to his comment to me, after I'd relinquished my role as financial planner, to become a professional speaker, coach and author. He said:

"David, now that you've left the world of financial services, I'd like to make a comment which might have seemed insensitive before.

*To be honest, **I don't think I've ever seen such a confusing and illogical way of being paid than that adopted by financial planners. I find it rather nonsensical!"***

And he went on to explain why.

Look at The Curious History

To understand what's behind Andrew's comments, it's worth examining how, and why, advisers and planners have been paid for many years.

It's a history lesson we tend to brush aside, ignoring the impact it has on the collective thinking of tens of thousands of us.

Eighteen years after the sea-change brought about by commission-reducing legislation in 2000, the vast majority of financial advisers and planners are still dependent for their livelihood on a singular type of payment.

Being paid a *percentage* of a client's investible assets still reigns as the financial underpinning to the whole financial planning community in the UK.

Whether this is right or wrong... whether this is good or bad commercially...
These questions are not so important at this stage.

What *is* important is *how* and *why* this method of reward came about.
What's the original commercial driver here? Who first set this agenda?

Let's agree on this one fact: no financial planner, nor any client, ever invented this percentage-of-assets commission model.

So, where did this model come from? Well, the answer to that is simple.

It was designed by *product providers* (manufacturers of financial instruments and investment groups) to ensure two outcomes:

→   The retail distribution of those investment products and instruments.
→   The capture and acquisition of consumers' investible assets.

In essence, that's it.

Listen to the language of investment groups even today. In conferences and seminars, they still talk about independent financial advisers and planners as *distributors* or *brokers.*

Obviously, they see nothing wrong with their language and perspective. This model seems a perfectly reasonable way of ensuring distribution of their products to capture investible assets, on which to then levy a management charge.

Of course, it's not difficult to see that the model also suited financial planners... once they had been weaned from the brutal front-end-loaded commissions of previous decades.

Admittedly, it took about 10 years for the percentage-of-assets news to get around the financial planning community. But eventually, all could see that this **Pricing** model created attractive results. You see:

THE FLIGHT OF THE SOUL MILLIONAIRE

→   It was easy to explain to the client.

→   It was easy to be paid this way.

→   It was more tax efficient for both client and planner.

→   It provided increasing stability to the revenue stream.

→   It forced firms to take a longer-term view.

→   It was easy to retire by selling an existing 'book of clients',
     which provided the acquiring firm with an almost guaranteed
     income stream.

> "What is the professional purpose of our business?
> Assuming it's financial planning... why are we being
> paid for something else?"

Try to Make Sense of The Baggage of Traditions

The first question arose when many financial planners started to question the morality and logic of this percentage-of-assets method. They declared that it wasn't merely simple; it seemed too simplistic.

They pointed to the ethics of advising a client who has, say, £5 million to invest, and charging that client in exactly the same way as another client with £500k. In both cases, the tradition was to take 0.5 percent (typically) of the client's investment portfolio.

The question asked was this:

*"Did the time, the risk and the complexity of working with the larger portfolio really justify charging that client **10 times** the fees charged to the client with the smaller portfolio?"*

Possibly. But unlikely.

The second question coming from advisers and planners, and arising more frequently in recent years, might sound like this:

"Is our firm positioning itself as financial planners? Or are we saying to the market that we're mainly about investment management?

If it's the first... then why is the bulk of our revenue dependent upon the second? If it's the second... do we have the education, experience and expertise to justify that position?

In other words, what is the professional purpose of our business?

And once we're clear about that, assuming it's financial planning... why are we being paid for something else?"

Yes, there are some notable businesses (like McDonald's) that sell one thing (burgers and fries) yet admit to being in business to do something quite different (McDonald's owns one of the world's most lucrative real estate portfolios).

Nevertheless, the question above is a valid one.

The third question is directed at the way that many advisers still hang on to the original remuneration structure created by product providers.

It's the old *3%+ 0.5%* model.

That is to say...

→   You take *no* remuneration for giving your initial *advice*, even though advice is what the client approached you for.

→   You take *3%* of the client's investible assets when you implement various financial instruments, even though implementation is the least important and least valuable activity, in the eyes of most clients.

→   You take *0.5%* of the client's investible assets each year – whatever you do, or don't do, to justify that amount in the eyes of the client..

Many now ask, *"Where exactly is the logic in that remuneration model?"*

→   *"Where's the logic in a model where, every time a new element of advice is given, the most money is taken from the client for the least valuable activity?*

→   *Where's the logic in a model where the quality and relevance of your advice is not rewarded... until you've completed the activity that is least important to the client?*

→ *Where's the logic in a model where remuneration is heavily based on the implementation of products... in a profession where the majority are loudly and proudly proclaiming that their role and ethos is **not** to sell products?"*

During 15 years of interviewing and coaching, I've heard the strangest, most confused arguments presented, in response to those questions.

Allow me to remind you that:

→ What we're *not* necessarily discussing here is what's right or wrong.
→ What we *are* discussing here is developing a business framework based on a solid foundation of relevance and logic.

Nevertheless, the percentage-of-assets model does carry some weight as a commercial argument. In addition, having built a whole industry on that model, there is, unsurprisingly, significant political weight and influence behind maintaining this status quo.

Meanwhile, sophisticated and experienced investors have grudgingly accepted *"this is the way it works here"*.

> Listen to the language of investment groups even today. They still talk about Independent Financial Advisers as Distributors or Brokers.

Rise Above The Fixed Mindsets

If you've been around almost as long as me… this whole situation is reminiscent of the film *Fiddler on The Roof.*

One of the timeless songs from that film is *Tradition.* Again and again, the hero, Topol, is forced to face the fact that his village's beloved traditions are not dealing well with the reality of his present world.

Tradition is a fascinating force on cultures and communities. What *Fiddler on The Roof* showed is that generations can continue a tradition… without ever stopping to ask:

→ *"How did this tradition start?"*
→ *"Why do we still continue it today?"*

The other intriguing influence of traditions is how they eventually interweave themselves with truth, until it's difficult to separate the two.

So it is with financial services and the subject of commissions and fees.

After so many years of accepting 0.5%-of-assets as the benchmark for charging clients for ongoing services, I've heard many proclaim this formula and percentage as *"fair"*. Consequently, they proclaim that charging more than this (perhaps double) is *"unfair"*.

How curious. We all know that 0.5% is merely an actuarially calculated figure, designed to attract and reward distributors of services and products.

The figure was never calculated to reflect a financial planner's skills. Neither was it calculated to reflect quality of work, nor the time and resources spent on that work. So, there's absolutely nothing *fair* or *unfair* about that figure, 0.5%.

Consequently, there can be nothing fair or unfair about charging *more* than that figure.

Behold, the power of tradition in fixing the mindset of a community!

> Value is not held within your service, your Product. Instead, value – what is **valuable** – only resides within the hearts and minds of your clients.

Bring Yourself Up To Date (And Create Further Confusion)

The confusion now arises as advisers try to move away from this simplistic model.

As they challenge it, the views start to multiply, and the strong differences in the community start to show. However, there appears to be agreement regarding the three distinct stages in the work of a financial planner, particularly when working with a new client.

The three distinct stages are:

1. **Stage 1:** the Advice Process
2. **Stage 2:** the Implementation Process
3. **Stage 3:** the Ongoing Planning, Accountability and Review Process

Each of these stages can naturally attract a separate fee, if desired.

You'd think that understanding there are three distinct stages to serving a client would make life easier and clearer, wouldn't you? Instead, these stages have merely added to the confusion and contention.

In the Advice Process:

→ Some firms believe that the Advice Process should be charged on a time-costed basis. That is to say, the time spent, by anyone in the team, on a client's Advice Process should be estimated or monitored. An hourly or daily rate should then be applied, and this will inform the minimum fee billed to the client.

→ Others believe that time-costing requires far too much micro-management. So, from past experience, they estimate a minimum and approximate cost for that type of task. They find a 'project fee', or 'flat fee', much more sensible.

→ Others don't charge for the Advice Process itself. They charge a fee for the resulting financial plan. Again, firms estimate the time and complexity likely needed to create the plan, and they attach a minimum fee to this work.

→ Meanwhile, there are other firms that won't charge at all for the Advice Process or the creation of a financial plan. Their intention is to recoup their investment of time, energy, skill and resources during the Implementation Process.

In the Implementation Process:

During this stage, the same differing methods above are used.

→ The most common is still the percentage-of-assets model.

→ But using time-costed fees for this process is quite popular too.

In the Ongoing Planning, Accountability and Review Process:

This stage probably attracts the greatest passion, the loudest voices and the widest differences of opinion, so:

→ Should this stage be time-costed?

→ Should it be a minimum flat, or fixed, fee?

→ Should it continue to be the good old percentage-of-assets model?

And so, the arguments rage.

I wonder what the public really think about this shambles; not to mention the noisy, inter-profession arguments displayed online?

Look at Different Questions For a Different World

It's time I was completely open about my reasons for raising all of these questions, and for asking you to examine the baggage of history being handed down to you.

Let me now make my views more transparent, by asking some questions.

A few years ago, in the middle of the upheaval caused by the Retail Distribution Review, I asked my financial planning clients I was coaching these questions:

→ *"If you knew that clients would willingly pay you a genuine fee, worth (at least) as much as you're currently being paid, and irrespective of their investible assets... what would that mean to your business?"*

→ *"If you knew you were completely immune from the sort of attacks being made on product/investment-based commission that happened a few years ago in the Netherlands... what would change for you?"*

→ *"If you knew that clients would pay you handsomely for your life-focused financial planning relationship – quite apart from any investment management... what would that mean?"*

My questions are driven by my experience in the most recent years of interviewing, coaching and consulting. This has highlighted two facts:

→ Most advisers have no idea whatsoever of how to sustain a business that is not being paid a percentage of a client's investment portfolio; and

→ Most financial planners I've spoken to would *love* to create a world where they can both sustain – and multiply – their ongoing revenue *without* dependence on this asset-based model.

Those reasons, those questions, that view are the driving forces behind me sharing a new model of Pioneer Pricing with you.

Become a Highly-Paid Pioneer: Approach Your Pricing Differently

By now, you'll be in no doubt that the last thing a **Pioneer** will do is follow the herd.

What Pricing Pioneers recognise is that receiving higher-than-average fees has little to do with pursuing high-net-worth or high-income clients.

Being paid higher fees than your peers, for the way you serve clients, has far more to do with:

→ Recognising how much clients will pay for what they really, *really* want; and

→ The way your service, your **Product,** complements and enhances important aspects of your clients' lives.

The question on your mind is probably, *Yes, but...*

→   *What do those firms **do** that pushes fees to multiples of the norm?*
→   *And how do they do it?*

So, let's have a look at both of those questions right now.

The most helpful experience I've gained in understanding the answers to this age-old question was when I stepped out of the financial services sector altogether. After 20 years as a financial adviser and fee-based financial planner... I wanted to see if there was life outside of the financial services sector.

I discovered that the world outside is alive, thriving... and more advanced. To my chagrin, I found most small and medium-sized businesses I interviewed were practising better leadership skills, better strategic thinking and better use of technology.

I also found that the thinking behind charging consultancy and advice fees was more robust, consistent and logical outside of the financial services industry.

One lesson, for which I'll be forever grateful, was discovering how other professions structure their fees, and what components go into that mix.

I'm going to share that with you now.

Once you see the logic behind that lesson, you'll be in possession of knowledge that will transform how you think about your professional worth and your remuneration. Forever.

Escape The Past: Study The Four Components of Any Professional Fee

Whichever profession you care to think of... there tend to be four main components, or driving forces, behind deciding upon a fee structure.

Let's examine the first three components

- → Component 1   Time-costed or cost-plus
- → Component 2   Expertise
- → Component 3   Risk

These are the components that drive the thinking of most professionals, such as accountants, solicitors, doctors, dentists. Their thinking sounds like this:

Component 1: Time-costed or Cost-plus

"Each member of our team is a costly resource.
Their time is part of that precious resource.

Therefore, we'll keep in mind the revenue we need to earn this year. Then we'll see how much billable time each member of our team has available this year.

This will tell us how much we need to charge for each team member, when working on client projects.

Finally, we'll add a profit margin to this hourly or daily figure."

Comment: This can be a brutal way of working. Ask any solicitor about how they try to maximise their billable hours. Ask them again how severely it shreds their health, and the time left for family life.

Since there are only so many hours in the day, there is a natural ceiling on how much revenue can be created.
You either try to pack more and more higher-value client work into each day...

Or you must steal more and more hours from your personal life, to maximise your firm's revenue.

Component 2: Expertise

"Each member of our team has a different level of knowledge, skill and expertise. Obviously, the greater and more specialised that expertise... the more each client must expect to pay.

This is not only because the expertise has the capacity to make a greater positive impact on the client's situation, but also because that expertise is rarer, more costly to acquire and costs our firm more to retain."

Comment: This has great advantages over the Time-costed or Cost-plus Component.

Obviously, the two tend to be combined in most firms. Also, there is a great attraction in developing an unusual type, or depth, of expertise. Clients will naturally pay more to a specialist.

What's more, it allows firms to move away from the race-to-the-bottom competitive **Pricing** game.

Component 3: Risk

"The more complex your situation and requirements, the higher the level of skill required to work with you, as our client.

Not only is this complex work more consumptive of our firm's time, energy and resources... this complexity also attracts a higher level of financial risk to our firm, and we need to ensure that we're covered for this risk.

All of these elements need to be reflected in our fee structure."

Comment: Of all components, this is the most negative in the message it sends to clients. In essence, you're saying that, *"We have to cover ourselves in case you sue us!"*

Not an attractive positioning statement. Nor is it a comforting contribution to the trust you wish to build with the client.

> You'll also reduce your blood pressure, by no longer fixating about how many items of activity you feel driven to perform, to justify your fees.

That's all well and good.

THE FLIGHT OF THE SOUL MILLIONAIRE

But what about Component 4? What happened to that?

Ah, yes! It's the fourth component that I wish you to concentrate on most fully.
Because, in my view, it's this component that holds the biggest promise... for both you and your client.

This fourth component is where Pioneers are streets ahead in their thinking about Pricing their Product.

Component 4: Value
This is, by far, the most powerful Component of all.

It's the same as the Value we discussed in the chapters on *Purpose* (Heartfelt Values) and *People*.

It's recognising that Value is not held within your service, your **Product.**
Instead, Value – what is *valuable* – only resides within the hearts and minds of your clients.

It's remembering that Value is viewed differently by each type of client.
So, discovering what your Ideal Clients would really, really value is the responsibility of every business.

It's not so much a matter of you *adding* Value (another piece of inappropriate language), as it is a matter of you clearly *recognising* how your Ideal Client *perceives* value.

What Component 4 also demands of you is that you understand what Outcomes your Ideal Clients seek in their engagement with you.

By Outcomes, I mean, firstly, Tangible Outcomes (the kind that are measurable and perhaps visible) such as:

→ The simplicity and clarity you bring to their financial affairs, or
→ The years of working life you save them by demonstrating that they're closer to being financially free than they thought, or
→ The taxes you help them save as they pass their wealth onto future generations.

Yet it's also critical that you understand what would constitute desirable Intangible Outcomes (the kind that are about feelings), such as:

→ The sense of peace you give them that they're more in control of their future, or
→ The satisfaction they feel in providing generously for their extended family, or
→ The excitement of realising that they can pursue dreams they otherwise would have buried.

Once you recognise that it's *these* things your clients regard as High Value... then it becomes easier to focus your attention on working towards these Outcomes.

When your firm becomes skilled at articulating, and then delivering, these Outcomes, you'll be walking a different path to the rest of your peers.

You'll also reduce your blood pressure, by no longer fixating about how many items of activity you feel driven to perform, to justify your fees.

Herein lies the greatest fee multiplier of all

The greatest fee multiplier is:

→ Not how much you can bill for your time and resources (that's really all about you).
→ Not how well you can cover your rear end in case you get sued (that's also about you).
→ Nor how much effort you've spent in passing exams and developing your expertise (that, too, is about you).

No. The greatest fee multiplier, and the greatest Value, is the impact – the Outcomes – your service has in the lives (not just the money) of your clients.

When that principle becomes the heartbeat of your **Positioning, Product** and **Pricing...**
You'll take your revenue – and your business impact and culture – to a level few ever achieve.

Now Weave That Insight Into Your Pricing

What happens now that you have this new insight guiding you?

Even with this different perspective of Component 4 – Value – you still need to create your own fee structure.

The difference is, however, that you're going to be free of the trappings of history, tradition and a herd mentality. Your thinking can be clearer, guided by what your Ideal Clients see, rather than what your peers see.

So, let me provide some pointers, by looking at the distilled essence of real-life examples. As you study them, see if you can uncover what makes them so different.

I'm going to use the simple principles applied by my clients such as Richard, Matthew, Steve, Andy, Simon and, of course, Mary.

Almost without exception, they made these changes step-by-step, rather than attempt a wholesale revision. Like you, they needed to test and increase their confidence, because such a fundamental change felt scary.

→ **Firstly,** they recognised that the problem in raising their fees existed primarily in their minds. Fear and lack of confidence were the underlying forces.

→ **Then,** they resolved to test out their new-found insights on *new* clients.
   Here they could gain confidence, and learn how to articulate their new thinking about Value without damaging existing client relationships. Typically, they found that being crystal clear about what Desired Outcomes they could create, gave them confidence to increase their **minimum fees** by at least 50 percent.
   These **minimum fees** became the key factor.
   It didn't matter what charging method they were using

at the time (whether percentage-of-assets or fixed fees), it was this minimum that allowed them to raise the bar and test the market.

→ **Next,** it wasn't long before 50 percent increases grew to 100 percent, then 200 percent, and more...

Only three factors limited the increase in those figures:

1. Their understanding of their true worth in the lives of their clients.
2. Their clients also understanding that worth.
3. The increasing confidence this gave to the adviser.

→ **So,** when the minimum was high enough to create a new, more sustainable financial future for the company... my clients made the biggest decision.

Some of them realised that this minimum fee allowed them to charge a fixed fee... whilst still creating more recurrent revenue than before.

Their business was now financially stronger.

Their Product was more relevant.

And they had differentiated themselves from the herd.

→ **Finally,** once they saw a pattern of acceptance by new clients, they examined whether they wished to apply their new fees to some, or all, of their existing clients.

That's how Pioneers learn to dramatically differentiate their Pricing and their Product.

> The greatest fee multiplier, and the greatest Value, is the impact – the Outcomes – your service has in the lives (not just the money) of your clients.

Why is All This (Positioning, Product, Pricing) Part of The Engage! stage?

There's a reason this stage in The Soul Millionaire Journey is called *Engage!*

The Purpose of all the Preparation and Pioneering is to start changing the nature and depth of our relationship with:

→ **Gatekeepers**
→ **Potential clients and, ultimately**
→ **Clients who have committed to paying for your services.**

When clients become deeply engaged with a business... their behaviour towards that business changes.

Not only do they tend to pay more – much more – for the privilege of such engagement, they also tend to become more ardent *evangelists* regarding their experience with that business.

And it is this attitude that can make them your most effective marketing team.

The problem is: how on earth can you tell when a client is deeply engaged with you and your firm? What signs do you look for?

Fortunately, there has been plenty of research done in this area in recent years. So, I'm going to present The Ten Signs of Deep Engagement to you.

Some of these signs you're ready to influence by acting on what you've learned so far on The Soul Millionaire Journey.

The other signs will unfold during the *Inspire!* and *Elevate!* stages of this Journey. Not only that, but you'll be given the tools to make all Ten Signs of Deep Engagement come alive for you.

As you learn and implement these tools... they will change the way clients perceive you, trust you, pay you... and help you in developing your business.

> The Deep Engagement of your clients correlates with the healthy growth of your firm.
>
> But the litmus test (of Engagement) is this... Have those clients provided referrals to you during the last three years?

The Ten Signs of Deep Engagement

1. They understand precisely why you love working with them, and people like them. You've made this clear even before you met.

2. They've provided input into how you can improve your service to them. They see that you have listened to their feedback and have implemented it... or at least let them know why you haven't.

3. They show the value of their engagement with you by *actively recommending* you to family, friends and colleagues.

4. Those recommendations become real referrals, not just passing comments. That's because you've engaged in educating them about the why and the how of introducing new potential clients to your firm.

5. They pay you handsomely, and certainly more than the industry average – perhaps double, triple or more.

6. They would be prepared to pay this handsome fee no matter how much wealth they bring to your engagement.

7. They see their communication with you as something that they look forward to, as a privilege and a joy. Reviews and meetings happen spontaneously, and not because you tell them it's necessary.

8. They understand your Passionate Purpose and your Heartfelt Values, and they approve and support them.

9. They have entrusted you with their hopes, dreams and yearnings; they believe this is as important as entrusting you with their money.

10. They recognise that your relationship with them is as much about their life as it is about investment performance, tax efficiency or some other monetary measurement.

Each of these Ten Signs of Deep Engagement is shown to correlate with the healthy growth of firms in your sector. They're not just nice-to-haves – they're drivers of a better future for you and your team.

Identify even the first three of the above in your client's behaviour and feedback... and you'll know that you're well on the way to an Engaged Client.

But, for me, the litmus test is this...

Have they provided referrals – personal proactive introductions – to you during the last three years?

The Thinking Bench

I remember talking to my eldest son, Adrian, about *branding.* At the time he was an executive chef, with responsibility for a number of restaurants.

I was asking him about the logo and visual messages being created for a new part of the business.

"Dad!" he exclaimed. *"You of all people should know that our brand goes far deeper than our visual image! It's everything we do, until the customer eats the product. And everything after that."*

Well, that told me.

These three subjects – **Positioning, Product** and **Pricing** – all go towards building your *brand*. The same is true of the principles within **Purpose, People** and **Preparation.**

Whether you understand it, believe it, or even like it... you already have a brand, which speaks to the world. The question is: what does it say?

Your brand is not just about coordinated colours, creative logos and captivating straplines. It starts with who you are, who you're becoming, and what you do to the lives of others.

Now, as the Hero of this story, your brand is about to be put to the test.

The next two stages in The Soul Millionaire Journey will do more than educate and inspire you. They'll test whether you're ready to start courageously acting on what you've learned so far.

Your ability to evolve and make a greater difference in other's lives will be tested by your clients... by your team... by your family... by your peers.

Your willingness to be patient as you walk through the Wilderness of practising new principles without demanding instant gratification... this will become part of your brand.

Your resilience as others question, and even oppose, your thinking… this will also become part of your brand.

Your grittiness in rising, like a small child, when you stumble… this too will become part of your brand.

Your brand – left unchanged – could keep you entrenched in the limits, frustrations and problems you've created.

Or – when you choose to change – your brand could catapult you into more revenue, more fulfilment, more influence and more joy in the work that you do and the business that you create.

You can go back to what was cosy and familiar in that feathered nest you've created. Or you can Soar, risking the buffeting of the winds, and so change your world… starting with you.

The choice is yours.

What Have You Learned?

→ What are the key points of your service for which your clients pay fees?

→ How much of your revenue depends upon Advice? How much on Implementation? And how do you separate the two in your client's mind?

→ If legislation changed in three years' time… and NO revenue could be taken from an investment product… how would this impact your business?

→ Which of the Four Fee Components do you use? Time-Cost, Expertise, Risk or Value?

→ What's your rationale for using percentage-of-assets as the basis for your financial planning fee?

→ How do you believe fee structures will change in your sector in the next five years?

→ In your view, will this change be driven by regulators, or by your peers?

What Will You Do Now?

→ What ideas from this chapter will you be discussing with your team in the coming weeks?

→ What will you do about ascertaining what Value means to your clients?

→ What would you need to do to increase your minimum annual fee by 50 percent in the next 12 months?

→ What is stopping you *doubling* your minimum annual fee in the next 12 months?

STAGE 3

INSPIRE!

What You Need to Know about The Inspire! Stage

Wendy and I love going to the cinema for our date nights.

Each year, there are one or two films where, as the closing credits roll, we want to stand up and clap. Sometimes we do, even if we're the only ones in the whole audience doing so.

There we watch, and gape at, stories of lives, tales of triumph against impossible odds – all of which inspire us. There we see depictions of wonder and majesty and glorious courage in the midst of frustration, disappointment and heartbreak.

These stories lift us, they renew our faith in the unconquerable **Possibility** of our souls. We leave that place of entertainment with hope still rising in our hearts.

What's interesting is that there are people we meet who have that same effect upon us. In their presence we feel inspired:

→   Not because of any celebrated talent or skill they might possess.
→   Not because of the clever things they say or advise.
→   Not because of how they make us feel about *them* and *their* life.

Rather, we feel so inspired... because of how they make *us* feel about *ourselves* and the possibilities in *our* lives. Because of who we wish to become, merely by having associated with them.

We leave them, to return to our daily round, but now with hope running through the spring in our step, and in the brightening of our countenance.

They are rare, these individuals. We all know them when we meet them, even if we don't know why we know. Few forget them afterwards. The memory of them lingers long in our spirits.

The question is this: **Are you such a person? Is your business such a place?**

And, if not so today... **would you wish to be?**

It is my experience that many of us carry within us the embryo of that person. More than we imagine, we have the capacity to inspire, to lift... to elevate the existence and lives of those we meet.

Yet, as financial planners, this happens only when we change our understanding of our professional role.

The *Inspire!* stage of The Soul Millionaire Journey will help you do just that. It will show you:

→   Why this – your ability to *Inspire!* – is more than possible.
→   What happens when you turn your role on its head and set aside some of the lessons you've learned.
→   How you can change your approach, and so inspire others in the ways I've discussed.

The key to all of this? The key is the coming together of two complementary skills:

→   **Financial planning and...**
→   **Coaching!**

Currently, the financial services industry calls this coming together *life planning* or *lifestyle planning*. Whatever you call it, the influence is unquestionable.

Possibility And Power

We'll examine this combination in two consecutive steps, which will be covered in the next two chapters:

1. **Possibility**
    You'll come to understand why few in your profession have appreciated the potential of their role to change lives. But only when that role is played to the full.
    You'll also discover why *you* might be the one getting in the way of your client's dreams and aspirations... because of your eagerness to demonstrate your skills as a financial planner.
    You'll see how the skills of Coaching are a natural fit with the profession of Financial Planning. More importantly, these skills will help you see your work through completely new eyes.
    You'll become clear on why integrating these new skills is directly linked to your firm's ability to serve better, to enjoy more fulfilment... and to be paid more.

Just as in the original Hero's Journey don't be surprised to find that your new approach to client relationships unsettles those who don't understand the changes in your behaviour.

Indeed, I've witnessed cynical public attacks by other financial planners, on those who've tried to explain how their businesses have blossomed because of this new combination of skills.

Yet, you'll make different friends, as you join a different and fast-growing community. This community will take your profession into a future that old-school financial advisers and today's financial planners will find unrecognisable.

To help you convert the surprise of others into a whole new level of trust and engagement... the second step will provide you with unusual competencies.

2. **Power**

In this step, we'll take the principles of **Possibility,** and design some practices.

We'll look at examples of the **Power** flowing from the frameworks, techniques and tools that are part of Coaching. We'll look at the *how.*

More importantly, we'll see why it is not *your* **Power** that is most important in this development of relationships. This is not really about *you* at all.

This is about you helping your clients to access *their* **Power.**

Their Power of imagination, creativity, intuition.

Their Power to resurrect buried dreams, to give substance and roadmaps to aspirations.

Their Power to convert hope to Tangible Outcomes, as they work in partnership with you.

You'll understand how to move from seeking superficial and two-dimensional facts and figures... to recognising what is behind all of those.

You'll see how – from the first conversation – you can change their perception of who you are and what you do.

You'll provide your clients with a deeper way of working with you and your firm. A way which will significantly raise your value, and thus your fees, in their eyes.

You'll also learn that these same Coaching skills will develop trust and engagement within your team, at a speed that defies business convention.

Chapter 12

Possibility

Here you'll see what happens
when you open your client's eyes
to what is possible in their life.

You'll also start to understand
why your eagerness to give advice
might be the factor that is getting
in the way of your client's future.

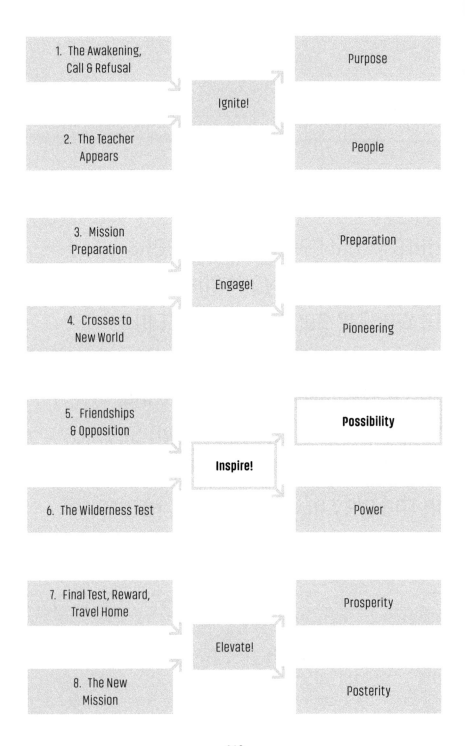

Make Meetings More Meaningful

Steve had been given the unusual opportunity of buying out his former employer.
In doing so, he was making the transition from young paraplanner to financial planner and boss.

We'd been touching base for a while as he became engrossed in the process of taking over the business. I found him a gentle, kind individual. But he seemed to lack the confidence needed to be a business leader, rather than a follower.

One day he phoned me, upset at being rejected by a strong-willed potential client. They had clearly taken control of the meeting agenda. They had laid down all the rules of engagement, won the investment arguments. They had satisfied their ego.

"Right!" said Steve. *"That's not happening to me again. So, I'd like you to coach me."* He went on to say, *"I have listed 14 life and business objectives I feel I'd like to fulfil during the next three years."*

I'm often amazed at people's expectations of this coaching process.

"But, first of all," he continued, *"I'd like to learn to do what you do. You know, to coach like you. I'd like to get clients to focus on what really matters, instead of them setting an academic agenda about investment performance and the cost of my services."*

That was the start of a fascinating and joyful coaching relationship.

269

Yes, Steve did achieve 12 of his 14 aspirations and goals (the other two eventually proved to be unimportant). But that isn't what matters in this discussion. What's more important is *who* Steve became in the process.

He became confident at going beyond the first problem that clients presented to him... and discovering the real problem.

He became supremely confident in *not* trying to add value by displaying his knowledge and wisdom. Instead, he learned the **Power** of gently asking more meaningful, searching and incisive questions.

For example, a couple approached him having recently received a sum in excess of £1 million. This had been both a pleasant surprise and a source of confusion for them.

Rather than dive into investment solutions, one of Steve's early questions was: *"How do you believe this is going to change your life?"*

"Wow!" responded the husband. *"That's such an obvious question. But a good one. To be honest, we've never asked ourselves that, until now."*

Steve found that, with such questions, he no longer needed smart sales presentations to convince potential clients of his professional worth. Clients expressed delight, and were visibly moved, as conversations with Steve took them in unexpected, more meaningful, directions.

> "I've just witnessed the power of coaching: the catalytic use of questions, enabling the human mind to travel one million miles in five minutes!"

Master Your Craft, Change Your World

Steve's breakthrough in confidence came when I directed him to one of my coaches (yes, every good coach has a coach if they're serious about their craft), for a three-day course. In large measure, the course was designed to help executives and business owners improve the quality of decision-making in their organisations.

I regard the course facilitator, Jane Adshead-Grant, as nothing short of extraordinary: used to working at a senior level in complex corporate environments. I've seen business leaders solve knotty problems within 30 minutes of speaking with her – problems they'd wrestled with for months, even years.

Observing such an experience, one business owner said, *"I've just witnessed the power of coaching: the catalytic use of questions, enabling the human mind to travel one million miles in five minutes."*

Yet, with all her brilliance, she was so impressed with Steve's coaching skills on the course that she went home and told her husband about this young financial planner. Before you could blink, they had appointed Steve as *their* financial planner.

You can't get a better accolade than that, as you develop a new skill. The Student becomes the Master.

Steve's newly-gained, relaxed confidence with clients is reflected in a few key characteristics:

→ His willingness to turn away any potential client who simply doesn't fit his Ideal Client description.
→ His increased minimum fee.
→ His reduced working hours, with more time at home with his family.
→ The healthy increase in his recurrent revenue.
→ His steady flow of Ideal Client referrals.

An investment group's business development manager, who knew Steve in his days as a paraplanner, commented: *"Steve is a man transformed!"*

Yes, he is.

That's what's Possible when applying the confluence of coaching and financial planning.

As mentioned at the beginning of this *Inspire!* stage, some call this confluence *life planning,* and others call it *lifestyle financial planning.*

I'm not sure it's important what you call it. What is important is the waking up of a profession to the **Possibilities** that this confluence creates.

Reveal What Matters Most

My coaching relationship with Nigel started in October 2007.

Nigel had left the bancassurance world and was working hard to make a living as an independent financial adviser. Each year he showed a marginal improvement in revenue. But he was exhausted, and not enjoying his work as much as he'd anticipated.

Our conversation was full of facts and figures, activities and productivity. But there was absolutely nothing different about what he was doing compared to thousands of others just like him. He was still behaving much as he had when working in the product-focused bancassurance world.

A *vanilla-flavoured practice* was the description we agreed upon for his previous occupation.

So, we met face to face for the first time; in or near Leeds, I believe. Halfway through our conversation I asked him what I call the Eulogy Question.

"Nigel, I want you to imagine that you're 83 years old. You've lived your life to the full, and last week you said 'Goodbye' to your family for the last time.

It's the day of your funeral.
Your two sons will each stand and, one by one, deliver their eulogy to you.

What would you wish them to say?"

I use this Eulogy Question whenever I feel that our conversation is skirting around What Really Matters to the person I'm coaching. I use it, because, all too frequently, business conversations deal with only the mechanics, the logic, the metrics – such conversations tend to strip out the humanity of what is, essentially, a conversation about people.

In stark contrast to that type of conversation, I'd ask you to recall any funeral you've ever attended. Think of what was said about that person, in whose memory everybody has gathered.

Do those who speak reel off that person's asset and income achievements?
Do they regale the congregation with the property or possessions that will be distributed in their will?
Do speakers quote their qualifications and the size of the business they built?

Of course not!

When I ask audiences *"Why not?"*, the answer that comes back every time is already hanging in the air before they've opened their mouths: *"Because those things are, ultimately, unimportant!"*

In Nigel's case, the result of the Eulogy Question was dramatic. Tears flowed immediately.

What he really wanted was:

→   That he would be seen as a role model for his sons.

→ That clients remembered him as someone whose professional skills changed their lives.

→ That his personal and professional community remembered him as someone whose life had been meaningful to them.

In the years after we'd concluded our work together, Nigel embraced coaching skills by immersing himself in the training provided by the Kinder Institute. It changed everything about his professional life.

Nigel went on to form his own business.
More importantly, he became a coach within the Kinder Institute, showing other financial planners how to bring more meaning and fulfilment to their work with clients.

"To change something, build a new model that makes the existing model obsolete."
Richard Buckminster Fuller

"Instead of fighting the industry," says Nigel today, *"I decided to lead by example, to show that you plan your client's life first, then you plan their money. David, you taught me to look through their eyes, their emotions.*

To confound the cynics, I've shown that this approach works commercially, not just as a way of advising at a more profound level.

By taking far more holidays than most... I've shown my clients that I am both credible and authentic. Not to mention that I'm more refreshed, recharged and reinvigorated for the benefit of my work with them.

Finally, I realised that changing the lives of 100 clients was one thing. Changing the behaviour of 100 financial planners... well, that could change the face of a whole industry, couldn't it?"

Wherever you review the work done by an effective coach or life planner... you'll see that lives have been transformed.

That's because coaching strips away the noise of busy lives, helping each of us to uncover – and act on – what matters most.

Face The Facts

I remember it well. It was in 1997 when I first became aware of the coaching principles, models and techniques that are now a normal part of my life. I was so excited by the **Possibilities** of a different kind of conversation that it didn't take me long to start integrating them into my work as a financial planner. So, in reality, as I write, I've actually been coaching clients for more than 20 years.

From clients' comments, it soon became clear that the depth of conversations they were having with me was not only unusual, but extremely valuable.

Jump forward 20 years...

The evidence of the impact of coaching in business is now overwhelming. A brief trawl of the internet shows just how much research has been done on business coaching effectiveness. The results are there, in the public domain for you to see.

In every possible arena of business, from improved leadership to deeply-engaged and higher-paying clients, coaching has left an indisputable track record.

UK corporations, and their global counterparts, now expect their coaching return on investment (ROI) to exceed five-to-one. In many recorded cases, in both large corporates and SMEs, ROI has been found to be many multiples of this – sometimes in the hundreds-to-one.

Monetarily, no matter what size your business, the impact on the bottom line can be considerable.

The evidence is both clear and considerable: coaching skills can have a profound positive impact on the way that people influence each other's thinking and behaviour.

Coaching skills can help individuals and teams dramatically change and improve where advising, consulting and mentoring fail.

That's because coaching strips away the noise of busy lives, helping each of us to uncover – and act on – what matters most.

Let's Dispel a Few Myths

If the positive outcomes of coaching in a business context are so obvious (and they are), **why then are many UK businesses so reluctant to run the risk of gaining from these possibilities?**

I've been considering this question for years. To find an answer, I've been observing workshop audiences and leadership teams to understand that reluctance.

Here are a few reasons I've noticed as prevalent within the financial services community:

→ *"I don't do touchy-feely."*
→ *"We're not counsellors, nor therapists."*
→ *"This approach is too American."*
→ *"We have enough plates to spin. We don't want to spend time learning about coaching as well."*

Let's look at these four statements in the light of research by Carol S Dweck. As a social psychologist at Stanford University, Dweck concluded decades of research on achievement and success by introducing the terms *fixed mindset* and *growth mindset* into the business world.

Dweck found that *fixed mindset* was an excellent way of describing those people who believe that their basic qualities – such as intelligence or talent – are fixed traits: innate and unchangeable. It is these people who spend their time proclaiming and proving their intelligence and talent, instead of developing them. They also believe that talent alone creates success, with minimal effort.

Fixed mindset people love to aim for measurable achievement; viewing failure as a permanent disaster. In fact, they do all they can to hide or avoid failure. Meanwhile, critical feedback feels to them like a permanent attack. Consequently, they choose directions and tasks where success is more likely, with risk minimised.

On the other hand, those with *growth mindset* believe that their most basic abilities can be developed through dedication, practice and hard work: intelligence and talent being just a beginning of achievement. This view of life creates a love of learning. It also creates a grittiness – an important ingredient for great accomplishment.

Growth mindset people see failure as an adventure and opportunity for change. They seek critical feedback. They embrace challenging tasks. They invest greater effort in creative risk, as they seek innovation and improvement.

It is *growth mindset* which boosts motivation, productivity and eventual success in any field.

Even before you've studied her work it's not difficult to see which of these two mindsets the above four statements emanate from.

Let's examine why that's so; let's see what the alternatives are. Let's bring the voice of reason into this conversation:

"I don't do touchy-feely."

I remember the summer's day well, as I sat listening to two leaders of a high-profile financial planning firm. The Managing Director was explaining to me why he wasn't enamoured by the approach to client relationships that I was suggesting.

"I don't do touchy-feely," he concluded.

To be honest, I'm not sure exactly what I said on that day. But (as is too often the case) I know what I wish I'd said. It would have sounded something like this:

→   *"Firstly, let's look at 'touchy'.*
You know, our clients aren't robots or vehicles of artificial intelligence. When we work with them, we're working with both their Intelligence Quotient (IQ) and their Emotional Quotient/ Intelligence (EQ). We're working with their humanity.
What could be more important in your work than so touching the life of each client... that their life improves following their engagement with you and your firm?
What could be more fulfilling than helping them change the way they think about, feel about and use this thing called Money... simply because your life touched theirs?
What could be more satisfying than to watch that money become a greater blessing in their life... because of the way you coach them to see it, think about it, feel about it and use it?"

→ *"Next, let's look at 'feely'.*

Surely, your long years of experience have taught you important lessons about what truly matters – what is essential – in life?

Surely, the most important decisions – even the most notable scientific breakthroughs – are seldom led by intellect? They're founded on what we feel, what our intuition tells us... long before our conscious thinking even knows what's happening.

Most of us are aware of the top two causes of divorce – after infidelity, money ranks as the second-highest cause of such heartache and dashed hopes. After cheating, it leads the field of relationship-destruction by a country mile.

On the one hand, in our culture, we gain great comfort from acquiring and possessing somewhat more money than we really need.

On the other, this instrument proves to be one of the most destructive forces in our most important relationships.

Why is this?

Perhaps it's because a human being's relationship with this means of exchange that we call money has seldom, if ever, been logical or factual.

Any study of this subject shows deep, often hugely dysfunctional, emotions, wrapped around what should be a matter of security and opportunity. Frequently this stretches back to childhood influences.

Consequently, to approach this subject as if it were based on facts and figures, logic and percentages, is to fly in the face of reality.

So, within or without a business context, 'feely' is probably the most important aspect of any human relationship."

"We're not counsellors, nor therapists."

Over the years, I have regularly found myself coaching management or leadership teams within which conflict is simmering beneath the surface. This is not unusual. Human relationships are complex creatures.

I remember one such team. Through careful coaching, we eventually brought those differences to the surface. Each member of the team then learned to be more open with the others in a way they'd never found possible in many years of working together.

It was a cathartic experience. It completely changed the dynamics of their work. It also had an enriching impact on their personal lives.

So, it became a matter of wonder to me when, having experienced the Power of coaching, the team refused to embrace that same Power in their own work with clients.

I came to understand they – for all sorts of reasons – were petrified that I was asking them to engage in therapy with their clients. Not just worried: petrified!

As they say in Yorkshire, *"There's nowt so queer as folk!"*

So, let's get clarity on this subject before we move on with our Journey.

Coaching, particularly in a business context, has its roots in a number of professional disciplines:

→ **Therapy**

Yes, there is the groundbreaking therapy-based psychology of people like Carl Rogers and Gerard Egan.

But therapy, counselling and clinical psychology are focused on fixing dysfunctionality.

Using coaching in your business role, you're not there to fix clinical dysfunctionality – that is a job for licensed therapists.

No, coaching deals with people who are basically already functional in their lives (although we might smile, when we see the behaviour of many people in business).

The emphasis in coaching is on removing whatever is blocking progress, and then revealing what is possible, as we look towards the future.

→ **Sports coaching**

Life coaching and business coaching have drawn many lessons from techniques learned in sports coaching.

However, much of sports coaching has to do with performance and a preoccupation with technique.

These are far less helpful perspectives when placed into the landscape of your business relationship with clients and your team.

Nor are sports coaching techniques so effective when the perspective is the nature and quality of client relationships. This setting has far less to do with your *performance.* It has far more to do with your ability to help others see, think and behave differently, particularly when addressing their emotional relationship with money.

→ **Mentoring, Consulting and Management Training**

As a coach, I have learned a great deal from mentors, consultants and management trainers, when considering client relationships.

Learning from consultants, I've realised that my coaching can never be conducted in isolation, in a cosy client-coach bubble. Everything my business clients think and decide will impact other people...

Consultancy perspectives have taught me that to ignore these ramifications during my coaching can be irresponsible, and even ethically questionable.

In your role the same applies. The decisions your clients make, as a result of your guidance and coaching, will tend to have ramifications on a number of other lives; perhaps many.

Coaching takes a more mature approach

For me, the beauty and Power of coaching lies in its ability to place two people in an adult-to-adult relationship.

Mentoring and consulting tend to adopt an adult-to-child/ adolescent relationship. That is, *"I know this stuff. You don't. So, listen up!"* They're both inherently rather *dependent* relationships.

Coaching, on the other hand, leans on the coach's skill in getting the coachee to think more brilliantly for themselves, to see and understand things they've never been able to before.

In this, it's the coachee, the client, who becomes the genius. Their mind doesn't need to be told. It is the coachee who learns to peel back biases, bigotries and assumptions that block their progress.

Their mind blossoms and moves towards brilliance in the coach's presence, and with the coach's skill.

To me, this is a far more mature, *interdependent* relationship.

And observing it in action is like watching magic unfolding in front of your eyes.

> Consequently, to approach this subject as if it were based on facts and figures, logic and percentages, is to fly in the face of reality.

"This approach is too American."

At face value, this comment may raise a smile. It may even smack humorously of thoughtless prejudice.

On the one hand, we accept that:

→   Our difference in the use of our English language can provide the source of many a joke.
→   The mental chewing gum of American TV keeps our two nations similarly visually occupied.
→   Pop songs in the UK and USA may be sung with a similar inexplicable nasal whine, evident since the 1960s.
→   We even find ourselves being dragged by our children to the same brands of indigestible, cholesterol-pumping junk food.

On the other hand, it's not difficult to see that there is a colossal cultural gap between our two nations.

At the time of writing, most people I've met in the UK stand back and observe the political scene across the Atlantic with emotions on a spectrum ranging from bemusement to horror.

How each nation views a foundational subject like the practice of Religion, and its relevance in everyday life, also leaves the other nation mystified.

Also, the considerable difference in perspectives and practices around work is not reconciled because we happen to be in the same line of business.

Add to that the lack of credibility, in a business environment, created by the strangely effete psychobabble sometimes adopted by UK-based life coaches, in trying to emulate some of their transatlantic counterparts.

Then it's not surprising that some cynicism has arisen as coaching has been introduced to UK financial services by coaches from the USA.

It might also be true that it is culturally alien, particularly amongst us men, to go deeper than the safe, two-dimensional surface of *"What are your goals and objectives?"*.

Yet how many advisers have come to me amazed (and proud) at the fact that clients say to them: *"I don't know why I'm telling you this. I haven't shared these thoughts with anyone else in the world, not even with my [spouse/partner/family/closest friends]!"*

Or how many advisers have excitedly forwarded emails to me, laden with praise like this: *"I'm not sure what we would have done, had we not met you. You've saved us five years of slogging away at work that we no longer enjoy."*

What cannot be argued is the measurable commercial and positive emotional impact that this *American* coaching has had on those UK financial services organisations that have actively integrated this skill.

Nor is there any longer much debate about the global impact that coaching – when actively supported at board level – can have on a business's tangible and intangible performance.

Add to that the fact that there are now at least 34 coaching master's degrees provided by UK universities.

Moreover, consider the fact that leading UK business brands see leadership, management and supervisory coaching as a normal part of their people-development strategy.

In other words, the global application and relevance of coaching skills is no longer open to question here.

What is definitely in question is the time it has taken for small and medium-sized businesses in the UK to accept the abounding evidence surrounding them.

As a response to the *"too American"* statement... I'll leave the final word to Sir John Whitmore.

Sir John was a champion racing car driver in his 20s.
He went on to build and lead a large agribusiness, a product design company, a Ford main dealership and two sports schools.

He gave up leading his businesses, however, in order to study psychology.

He became a pre-eminent thinker in leadership and change... and one of the most respected organisational leaders and authors in the international business coaching world.

Here's his comment: *"How can you call yourself a leader in this brave new world, if you do not have coaching skills as part of your leadership?"*

**"We have enough plates to spin.
We don't want to spend time learning about coaching as well."**

Buried in this statement – this rationalisation – is the biggest opportunity of all for your firm.

Yes, you're busy. In an ever more complex world, we all have a great deal of possible actions we face each 24-hour day.

The question is: which of your decisions today will make the greatest impact tomorrow? Because not every decision facing you will have the same weight.

The universe of business is violently imbalanced. There will always be decisions to be made, skills to learn... some of which will outweigh all others by a geometric factor.

Coaching is just such a skill.

I – and many others – have observed this skill change the goalposts in two areas of this business sector:

→   Financial planning
→   Leadership.

In financial planning, the commercial results show:

→   There's deeper, more passionate Client Engagement and trust.
→   This is reflected in a more consistent flow of quality referrals.
→   Clients will pay more for the services they've agreed to.
→   There's less need to justify those fees by increased levels of service activity.
→   Revenue per employee shows more than marginal improvement.

In leadership, the results show:

→   Less busy-ness in the business, which ensures noticeably less stress.
→   Whole teams become more engaged with clients, rather than depend upon the personality of the financial planner.
→   Quality of service improves, because of a whole-team commitment.

THE FLIGHT OF THE SOUL MILLIONAIRE

→ Teams are more aligned with the vision and mission of the leader(s).

→ Teams are more fulfilled, and evidence greater joy in their work.

→ There's lower employee turnover and less absenteeism.

→ There's reduced conflict at all levels of the business.

→ Meetings are more productive.

And so, the list continues...

"How can you call yourself a Leader in this brave new world, if you do not have coaching skills as part of your leadership?"

Sir John Whitmore

Still not convinced?

I've already provided you with real-life examples of just some of the outcomes of coaching.

Here are two more:

The first story...

I followed the progress of one corporate coach, who was also heading a human resources (HR) learning and development team.

His task was to introduce coaching into the Leadership Development Programme of a multinational organisation.

Not surprisingly, his team met resistance from leaders in some areas of the business. *"Our sales techniques work. My team gets revenue results. Why bother changing now?"*

So, using his resources wisely, he decided to *'Go Where The Energy Is'.*

In less than two years, the HR team reviewed the UK's different divisions, comparing the Leaders-Are-Coaches (LAC) division with the rest.

In more than a dozen factors, employees' attitude towards the group, and towards their work, had *measurably* improved in this LAC division.

But even more intriguing, the *increase* in employee positive attitude in this LAC division was mirrored by a similar *decrease* in employee positive attitude in those other divisions.

Here's a question....

What would happen to *your* firm, if your whole team became more passionate and more positively engaged in both your organisation... and the work they were undertaking?

Is that just spinning another plate?
Or is there perchance something that you're currently not yet enjoying?

The second story...

It didn't take long for me to become impressed by Jane's work ethic, and her ability to simultaneously see both the big picture and the detail. (Incidentally, we're not talking about coach Jane Adshead-Grant here. This is yet another Jane.)

In her role as Support Manager, everybody from top to bottom in the firm depended on her having her finger on the pulse. Internally and externally, everybody (except the MD) could see that Jane ran the whole firm.

Of course, there's a double-edged sword to that status in any business. Jane was run ragged. Everybody saw her as the fount of all knowledge, the source of every answer, the solution to every knotty problem.

That is, until Jane became a dedicated student of leadership coaching.

Gradually, she was able to get her team – as well as the advisers – to think for themselves.

With this better thinking, the quality of decisions improved no end. Productivity and excellence – not activity – became the order of the day.

Jane then helped others to learn about coaching, particularly those whom she saw as the rising stars in her team.

Today, coaching skills are a driving force throughout the team. Using its techniques to discuss strategy and tactics is the norm.

There's less stress, better quality revenue and more focus on developing people – not just using them as functions to fulfil the ambitions of the leaders.

Jane is now a director of the firm. With her, those rising stars have already become the new generation of decision makers and leaders.

Coaching is not just another plate to spin.

Coaching is the pole that enables all other plates to spin longer, with greater control, more certainty, and with less stress, less frantic energy and fewer breakages.

Coaching enhances the way you lead... the way you plan... the way you advise.

It allows you to have greater impact in all of these areas... whilst working with greater ease to create that impact.

Being a financial planner who is more coach-like, creates a more powerful skillset and more opportunities to serve your client than most financial planners will ever have experienced.

This is why we call coaching *the great revealer of possibility.*

A Final Word on Possibility

If you think that the only work your profession enables you to perform is tidying up clients' confusing financial affairs... or saving them a wodge of tax... then you're underestimating what's possible.

Most of the people you meet are bowling through their working life carrying a backpack full of regrets and unfulfilled hopes.

One of the tender parts of my ministry is spending time with people who are not far from their last breath.

Listening to them, I get to see life from such a magnificent perspective, spread over seven or eight decades. The stories they have to tell! Yet, invariably, there are holes in their heart which, being busy with work, have never been filled.

The Six Regrets of The Dying

One of the popular books that has brought these regrets to the attention of a younger generation is Bronnie Ware's *The Top Five Regrets of the Dying.*

She summarises her work as a palliative nurse with this simple list of statements, provided by her patients and clients:

1. *"I wish I'd had the courage to live a life true to myself, not the life others expected of me."*
2. *"I wish I hadn't worked so hard."*
3. *"I wish I'd had the courage to express my feelings."*
4. *"I wish I'd stayed in touch with my friends."*
5. *"I wish I'd let myself be happier."*

I would add one more, based on my own experiences in ministry:

6. *"I wish I hadn't settled for less than my dreams."*

You might ask, *"But what has this list of Six Regrets to do with me, a financial planner?"*

To which I'll respond:

"Tell me how many other professional roles allow you to get so close to sensitive subjects like money, and the impact that ignorance or wisdom, in using that money, can have on clients' lives?"

I would also add:

"Tell me how many other professional roles cover such a wide range of intimate aspects of a client's life, business, family and other close relationships?"

This list of Six Regrets is a fair reflection of what many of your clients might say to themselves when they draw close to their last breath. Unless something changes in their today, that is.

"If you can be a catalyst in helping to instigate that change...
If you could do that as part of your normal working day...
...why on earth wouldn't you?"

Because what coaching empowers you to do is:

→   Handle these sensitive and important subjects with much
     greater vision, insight and finesse.
→   Help clients connect their money with meaning and **Purpose**
     in their lives.
→   Show them how their fears and their lack of understanding
     are smothering their hopes and derailing their possibilities.
→   Help them identify what is truly important (and it's not
     portfolio performance).
→   And then, with science, perspective and skill... help them
     to improve their *circumstances* – not just their *money*.

You can help people live lives with fewer regrets.

Almost every financial planner I meet tells me they want to *"make*
a difference".
Well, you really can make a greater difference through the conduit
of your business.

But first, you need to earn that right by learning the right skills.

Come With Me to
The Thinking Bench

It's not often that I turn to popular singers as a source of inspiration and courage.

However, Jamaica's Bob Marley expressed an uplifting concept in one of his songs.

He believed he could combat racism and hate by injecting the world with uplifting music. In doing so, he believed we could also inject Love through that music.

One evening, he was scheduled to perform in a peace rally, when gunmen came to his house, and shot him.

Two days later, he walked out on the stage, and he sang.

When asked, *"Why?"* he responded...
"The people who are trying to make this world worse are not taking the day off. Why should I?"

The song I'm thinking about is **Light Up the Darkness.**

You can change the history that has been passed to you as legacy in today's world of financial advice. Not all of that history is praiseworthy.

You really can Light Up the Darkness... making a greater difference... if you but change your own mindset about what is possible through the confluence of financial planning and coaching.

What Have You Learned?

→ If you knew that your professional skill could help clients live with fewer regrets... what would that mean to you? What would that change for you?

→ How do you keep clients focused on what really matters... rather than allowing them to be obsessed with investment performance and the cost of your services?

→ What methods do you use to get behind the problems first presented to you by clients... and then reveal their real problems and questions?

→ Have you ever found yourself saying, *"That approach is too American,"* or, *"I find that too touchy-feely?"* In what context did those comments arise?

→ What was the latest element in your business that – when adopted – created an ROI of greater than 5-to-1? What about 20-to-1?

→ In your role, with your clients or your team, do you see yourself as a consultant, mentor or coach? What is it about your behaviour that has led you to that view?

What Will You Do Now?

→ What could you do about introducing coaching skills into the financial planning and leadership roles in your firm?

→ How can you influence your clients, such that their later life has far fewer regrets?

→ How will you get clients to engage more fully with your team, and depend less upon your own time, energy, skills and personality?

Chapter 13

Power

This is where you take the **what** of **Possibility,** and structure the step-by-step **how,** to release the **Power** of coaching into your conversations with clients.

And you'll do this by saying less... asking more... and changing the way you advise.

Forever.

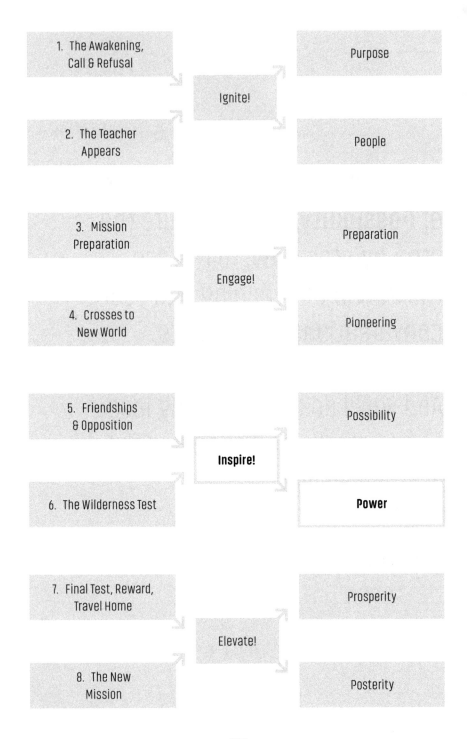

1. The Awakening, Call & Refusal		Purpose
	Ignite!	
2. The Teacher Appears		People
3. Mission Preparation		Preparation
	Engage!	
4. Crosses to New World		Pioneering
5. Friendships & Opposition		Possibility
	Inspire!	
6. The Wilderness Test		**Power**
7. Final Test, Reward, Travel Home		Prosperity
	Elevate!	
8. The New Mission		Posterity

How Can I Say This Politely? For Goodness Sake, Do Shut Up!

Coaching with Austyn can only be described as embarking on a breathless, wondrous adventure.

He epitomises all that I enjoy about working with the entrepreneurial souls I have had the privilege to meet – souls who commence every meeting with a page of 30 exciting, visionary ideas that have come to them during the last seven days.

I recently glanced at my 17 pages of notes from just two conversations with Austyn... there were enough ideas there to launch a dozen businesses!

Yet, what struck more forcibly was recalling what I didn't say. Because, in 11 hours of meetings, I only remember speaking for a total of 15 minutes... maximum.

Eight of The Best Superb Questions

I'll share with you now eight of my favourite questions, each of which I made use of during those 11 hours:

1. *"What would make this an excellent discussion for you?"*
2. *"What do you want to think about? And what are your thoughts?"*
3. *"What more do you think... feel... or want to say?"*
4. *"What do you want to achieve at this point in our conversation?"*

5. *"That's interesting. What's behind that, do you think?"*
6. *"Do you think that's true? Is it just possibly true? Or could that be an assumption you're making?"*
7. *"In order that, what...?"*
8. *"What's been most helpful to you in today's conversation?"*

They're not exactly complicated, are they?
Yet, used at the right point with a client, they move mountains.

The mind functions better when it can hear itself think.

Now, you could be forgiven for thinking that the genius-level, business-transforming ideas that flowed from Austyn were purely down to my astute questions. It would certainly stroke my tender ego to believe so.

The Power of silence

But the **Power**, the real **Power**, lay in the *silence – my silence –* whilst Austyn thought and spoke, and thought and spoke, and thought and spoke some more.

My contribution to Austyn's genius was to invest hours and hours of intense listening to Austyn's every word and emotion; and my absolute, almost reverent, **silence**.

Austyn said that being in that room together was like receiving extra light – light that chased away the shadows of doubt and fear and allowed him to see his business and life anew.

He went on to describe how his business could also be a beacon of light in the industry:

"A light that would illuminate the inadequacy and uninspiring service of other advisers."

And the words continued to flow...

"A light that would attract – think mesmerising glow – and fascinate new clients. Dozens of them. Perhaps thousands, if we wished."

Now he was unstoppable...

"A light that would show the way ahead, illuminating for clients the steps through the foggy confusing path of money... to a life of greater wealth, in the fullest, deepest sense of the word."

All rather poetic. But more than that, these were apt metaphors.

I've found that coaching, particularly when allied to other professional skills, can act like a prism: coaching takes what looks like white light and reveals the glorious colours behind what we think we see.

The other discovery Austyn made in these hours together was this wonderful two-part truth:

1. **The mind functions better when it can hear itself think.**
2. **The mind thinks more creatively in the presence of a perceptive listener.**

> Each person is waiting for the three-microsecond gap, when the others draw breath, and then they're right in there with a solution they're convinced will win the next Nobel Peace Prize.

If there's one prerequisite to developing this transformative **Power**... it is the need to let go of your consuming need to be heard.

It is the ability to listen like you've never listened before.

Many a financial planner has told me how superb they are at listening to their clients' wishes and wants. Yet, half an hour into our conversation, one thing is evident: they're not really listening at all, even on the odd occasion when I make a statement. They're simply waiting for the next opportunity to speak!

This is particularly obvious when they're joined in a meeting by one or more colleagues.

Then, what I observe is this:
Each person is waiting for the three-microsecond gap, when the others draw breath, and then they're right in there with a solution they're convinced will win the next Nobel Peace Prize.

Get Out of Their Way

Why is it so painful for us to stop talking, to stop pretending to listen, and to actually commit to hearing the person in our presence?

I've concluded that there are a number of forces working against us:

→ **Culturally, the odds are not in our favour.**
From our earliest playground years, we (men in particular) are taught to compete, to conquer and dominate, to be *top dog* or *king of the castle*.
This plays itself out in business conversations as we fight for airspace, for the improved ranking of our opinion, the **Power** to convince or the need to be right.

→ **We desperately need to feel in control. And admired.**
We feel in control of both conversation and relationship when giving our advice, demonstrating our knowledge, taking our stance or convincing others of our credibility.
We also like the praise that comes in response to our articulated wisdom, and as a consequence of our advice.
Listening and asking questions seem to flow contrary to all of that; when we're trying to do either, we feel as if we're totally out of control of the situation.

Yet, that is the point.

Because, the fact is… you're never really in control at all.

Instead, it's the mind and heart of the person(s) with you that hold all the trump cards:

→ The decisions will come from *them*.

→ The actions will come from *them*.

→ The biases and obstructive assumptions are inside of *them*.

→ The dreams are in *their* hearts.

→ The aspirations are in *their* minds.

→ The hopes, fears, frustrations and life lessons are in *their* soul.

→ The Aha moments will only have impact if they arise in *their own* thoughts and emotions.

Talk... persuade... coerce... and you're in danger of stifling all of that.

Listen, and the person in your presence will also feel valued and respected.
Or do you wish them to feel something other than that?

> They're not really listening at all. They're simply waiting for the next opportunity to speak.

Can you get better at this influential skill? Of course!

Like all skills, some education, followed by determined practice, can soon change your feeling of no longer being 'in control'. Indeed, you'll learn that you can guide and influence even more powerfully by just shutting up!

In doing so, you'll unearth causes, rather than symptoms, and truth, rather than assumptions. You'll learn that the **Power** of your curiosity can be greater than your intellect.

Pretty soon, your change in behaviour will change the way that clients, colleagues and loved ones feel when in your presence. That change can come about in mere days.

Lose This Habit. You'll Insert Genius And Trust into Your Client Meetings

The quality of the behaviour – and the results – in any business depends first on the quality of the thinking within that business.

Even the briefest consideration of this statement reveals it to be self-evident.

In large measure, the same can be said for our personal lives.

This is just one lesson that became clearer to me after studying Nancy Kline's *Time To Think* series of books. Thirty years of research and testing with business teams at all levels has given Nancy some alarming insights into the effectiveness – and ineffectiveness – of how people think when in each other's presence.

When the best ideas flow into a room or into a group of people... those ideas tend to have a measurable impact upon the lives of those present.

I've learned that these best ideas tend to flow even more readily in the presence of, what I call, Superb Questions and Brilliant Listening.

With clients, these principles, when brought to life, have a discernible effect on the outcomes of the client-planner relationship.

It follows that your responsibility – with your client, with your team, in your life – is to cultivate clear thinking within those in your presence.

Having said all of that, it is a matter of amazement that too many of us indulge in the destruction of that much-needed quality of thinking.

How do we do that?

We interrupt.
We interrupt each other's thinking and speaking.
We do it again, and again, and again.

For many of us, it's become an addiction, so deeply ingrained is it in our behaviour.

Helping leaders and planners to wean themselves off that addiction can be emotionally and physically painful for them.

I've watched board members squirm in their seats and start to perspire because I've asked them not to interrupt their colleagues. Some look as if they're about to have a most unpleasant accident.

You see, the greatest ideas are usually not the first to surface in our minds.

Therefore, interrupting a person in their thinking is guaranteed to block the most valuable ideas from surfacing.

If you're to practise the life-changing **Power** that your professional role is capable of, interrupting is something you cannot afford to do in your client conversations.

The greatest ideas are usually **not** the first to surface in our minds.

Again, we find that what goes on inside of us often smothers other people's ideas before those fragile ideas see light of day. We do this through:

→   Our desire to dominate.
→   Our yearning for recognition.
→   Our insistence on being right.
→   Our wish to do the other person's thinking for them.
→   Our concentration on forming our response to whatever we've heard so far.
→   Our assumption that we know precisely what the other person is about to say.
→   Our guess that what we have to say is more important anyway.

Research shows that some professionals, such as doctors, tend to interrupt every 18 to 30 seconds.

Sadly, research in the workplace also shows that men interrupt women far more frequently than vice versa. In fact, between 32 percent and 500 percent more frequently, depending on the business context.

I look at the five grown children whom my wife and I love... and I sometimes think back to their occasionally turbulent teenage years.

If there's one behaviour on my part that drove them wild (and raised the decibel level in the home), it was my inclination to interrupt them when I knew they needed some of Dad's deep wisdom.

My children taught me some stark lessons about the habit of interrupting. They saw it as rude. They saw it as arrogant. They saw it as demeaning. I make no apology for passing on those comments, undiluted, to my clients and readers.

Rest assured, you don't want a single one of these adjectives or adverbs to describe your behaviour with your clients and your team.

I believe that, when a person opens their life, feelings and dreams, to us... we're walking on sacred ground. Interrupting their thoughts with our brilliant solutions is like stomping on that ground with all the finesse of a lumberjack in hobnail boots.

In business, as in life, there are some ingrained habits that are helpful. Others are harmful. This one – interrupting – can suck the oxygen clear out of the room and snuff out the Power in your role before it's fully alight.

Beware The Man With One Book

"There's no one way of coaching, any more than there's one way of walking."

Sir John Whitmore

One of the healthy aspects of coaching, particularly in a business context, is the variety of psychological models and frameworks that have been developed and tested over the years.

Within financial services a number of these models have been tested too; however, at the time of writing, in the UK, I observe that only one has gained traction: that of the Kinder Institute of Life Planning.

When we consider why, **there seem to be four underlying reasons:**

1. The original model revolves around three, simple, memorable questions.
2. The three simple questions are merely the start – students learn that coaching requires the skill to use the questions at the *right time* in the process. This skill takes time, practice and support to learn and integrate.
3. The framework of questions has been mapped carefully across the whole financial planning process.

4. There is a train-the-trainers programme, which allows the philosophy to spread faster, and makes the business model more scalable and sustainable.

Now the three simple questions are nothing unusual. Most new coaches will have used them, or something remarkably like them, in the earliest part of their career.

So, it's actually the third reason – the carefully-mapped framework – that provides the **Power** and flexibility in remaining sensitive to the shifting context and emotions of any conversation.

Coaching, when allied to a skill like financial planning, requires that flexibility and nimbleness of thinking in a potentially complex discussion.

That doesn't mean that you need to learn scores of different questions. It *does* mean, however, that dependency on, say, just three questions, or one type of question, will almost certainly leave you floundering at some stage of the client conversation.

I remember once calling one Life Planning organisation to discover more about what they taught.

The consultant at the other end of the phone revealed his training, and naivety, when he said, *"If you use our questions, then you must follow all the questions and our process, just as we've designed it. Otherwise it doesn't work."*

I was both amused and dismayed.

Yes, there are some coaching models that are superbly effective when you can hold tight to the framework. But only someone in love with their own story would demand such a mechanical approach to such a transformative skill.

Of course, it's not surprising to find plenty of coaches and organisations that extol their own models and frameworks as *The One Right Way.*

And yes, I am aware that many organisations have created such models after decades of testing in different contexts and industries.

However, in most cases, such a stance is ultimately unhelpful to those wishing to integrate coaching skills into their existing roles.

What I believe is more helpful for our *Inspire!* work is to design a coherent, practical framework of questions that also provides you with the flexibility you need.

Empowered by such a framework, you can then develop the **courage** to ask your clients and your team questions that you know will be transformative.

Constructing The Framework: The First Meeting

In any business, it's the first detailed conversation, the first meeting – whether physical or virtual – that holds the most promise.

Constructed and conducted well, that first meeting will:

→ Create Trust at a speed that will surprise you.
→ Give permission for your Potential Client to be unusually open, even vulnerable.
→ Help them peel back initial information and 'symptoms', to reveal truths and causes that might even surprise them.
→ Open the gates for ideas, dreams, aspirations and hopes to flow... which have been buried by the pace of their lives.
→ Help your potential client to connect the dots between what they really, really want... and the life-changing Journey they can travel with you.
→ Confirm whether you want them as a client.
→ Precipitate them to take action if you do.

With that much on the line, we're ready now to construct a framework for that first Transformative Conversation.

Remember, this is just a framework; it's not *The One and Only* framework.

> I believe that, when a person opens their life, their feelings and dreams, to us... we're walking on sacred ground. Interrupting their thoughts with our brilliant solutions is like stomping on that ground with all the finesse of a lumberjack in hobnail boots.

Kickstart the conversation

Too often, we dither around during the first few minutes of a meeting, particularly if we've not met before.

We engage in trivial and meaningless social chit-chat...
We ask inane questions about the client "finding us easily", or whatever...
We build up to it...
We work our way towards it...

Seven Superb Questions That Create a Transformative Conversation

The Transformative Conversation gets straight to the point with...

1: The Ignition Question

The Ignition Question sounds like this:

"What would make this an exceptionally good meeting for you?"

Here are three alternative questions:

→ Influenced by Facebook: *"I wonder... what's on your mind?"*
→ Then there's: *"From your point of view... where's the best place for us to begin?"*
→ Leadership coach and author Nancy Kline's favourite would be: *"What do you want to think about, and what are your thoughts?"*

However they respond, and for whatever length of time, they're going to come to what seems like the end of their thinking. Don't be fooled: it never is the end!

So, whatever you do... never jump in with your '21 Best Financial Planning Questions', or your slick flipchart presentation, or whatever. Never.
Remember this is about: Superb Questions and Brilliant Listening.

There's a lifetime of treasure buried in that being sitting in front of you.
You just need to be patient and listen to their response to the next question.

Because the next question gives them permission to let their mind wander and wonder.

Elegantly simple as that question is... it helps them go on a journey to collect thoughts and feelings that have danced around them like butterflies, but without ever having been captured, or even noticed.

2: The AWM Question

This is definitely one of my favourites.

You simply ask: *"And what more?"*

That's it. *"And what more?"*

Then, close your mouth, open your ears, stop the chatter in your head... and listen. Brilliantly.

You might have to hold your breath for a while. But:

→　If you practise the courage to wait through the seemingly-interminable silence...

→　If you can quieten your ego...

→　If you can just hold your nerve...

Their mind will open a new gate... and even more fascinating, revealing words will flow through.

Here are three alternative questions:

→　The first alternative might be: *"Anything more that occurs to you?"*

→　Or perhaps, simply: *"Other thoughts?"*

→　A question developed by Nancy Kline: *"What more do you think... or feel... or want to say?"*

⇨　It's this question that led one business leader to say, *"I've just witnessed the power of coaching: the catalytic use of questions, enabling the human mind to travel a million miles in five minutes!"*

When you've allowed all of their responses to pour into the room, you'll reach the point where you're ready to pull together the strands of the conversation.

3: The Priority Question

At this stage, you're ready to help the client be more succinct and specific about which of all their thoughts feels more important than the rest.

The Priority Question sounds like this:

"Of those things you've discussed so far... what do you really want to focus on now?"

Here are three alternative questions:

→ You might say: *"Given all that you've just described... What is the one thing you really want to happen in your life, that's not happening yet?"*

→ Or perhaps: *"You've mentioned a number of things which sound important. I wonder which of those is the priority for you right now?"*

→ Or simply: *"Right now, what's the priority for you?"*

Remember, at this point, the agenda needs to come from them. Don't let your agenda get in the way of what they really, really want.

Meanwhile, for goodness sake, stop trying to *Add Value!*

Let *them* show you where the value in your relationship will really reside. Let *them* point to the one desire they'd most want to achieve right now.

Talking of Value, this is a perfect place to introduce...

4: The Value Question

This is a two-part question.

It's where they – not you – start putting a value on fulfilling a need, a desire, a dream, an aspiration that they – not you – have just 'placed on the table'.

The Value Question sounds like this:

"If you knew you could do that... how would life change for you?"

Here are three alternative questions:

→ The first alternative might be: *"If you knew you could do that... what purpose would that serve for you?"*
→ This one has proved effective for me: *"If you knew you could do that... what would that mean to you?"*
→ Then there's: *"And you'd want to do that, in order that... what?"*

Then there's the second part to the Value Question

Asking it clarifies, for both of you, whether what they've just said really is important, or whether it's just a whim, carrying little emotional weight.

The question sounds like this:

"And... what makes that so important to you?"

An alternative might be: *"I wonder... if you didn't do that... what then?"*

Once they've begun to articulate what's likely to be hugely valuable to them, it's time to help them connect the dots. That is, to make the connection between *what matters most* and their *money*.

Not surprisingly, there's a question designed to do just that.

5: The Connection Question

Gradually, the UK financial planning community is accepting the concept that their responsibility and opportunity is to help clients connect *money* with a sense of *meaning* in their lives.

The problem is, financial planners are so eager to practise this more enlightened way of thinking that they insist on showing clients this connection. The eagerness robs clients of the opportunity to think, and articulate the connection, for themselves.

So, yet again, here's a question that demands you get out of the way of your client's inherent genius.

To do that, first you refer to their money, or investment, or pension, or whatever they've brought to you for discussion.

Then, the Connection Question sounds like this:

"Now I'm curious... in your mind, what's the connection between this [money, etc.] and what you really, really want in your life?"

Here are three alternative questions:

→ One might be: *"How does this [money, etc.] you wish us to work with help with the [aspiration, dream, etc.] you've just described?"*

→ Then there's: *"To live the life you've described today, how much of this [money, etc.] will you need?"*

→ Or perhaps: *"If you knew you could do the things you've described today – without your money increasing in value at all – what would that mean to you?"*

Once you're clear that they're making that connection for themselves, it's time to move to Question 6.

6: The Spotlight Question

It's time to get them to start confirming your commercial relationship. Or at least to start reaching a conclusion about continuing the relationship you've started to develop.

You'll sense when the time is right to test the relationship in this way:

→ Do they think you can help them?

→ Or is investing further energy likely to waste time for both of you?

So, let's ask them. Let's put them, and their view – not yours – firmly in the spotlight. Remember, the **Power** lies in *their* thinking.

Your responsibility is to help them see what they didn't see before, and to say what they've never said. In doing so, they'll capture and clarify the jumble of thoughts and feelings flitting through their mind and heart.

The Spotlight Question sounds like this:

"Given all that we've discussed today, how do you believe I can best help you?"

Here are three alternative questions:

→ You could try this: *"What do you want to achieve at this stage of our conversation?"*
→ Or perhaps: *"What steps do you want to take now?"*
→ Or simply: *"How can I best help, do you think?"*

Before you conclude this line of discussion, it's important to create the right expectations of how you might work together. It's time to let them know that you're not there to do all the thinking and 'entertaining'. Rather, this relationship will work best when there's a partnership of thinking and acting.

7: The Partnership Question

You've reached the point where you're ready to agree:

→ *How* you might work together, and
→ *Why* you would both wish to do that.

This is not a matter of coercion, or even persuasion. You're not switching into sales mode. What you are doing is seeking clarification.

However, you're also alluding to a relationship that works best as a partnership.

The Partnership Question sounds like this:

"So, for our relationship to work for you...

...it would seem we need to accomplish the following (let's say three,) things in your life you've said you want most?

#1...
#2...
#3...

Have I understood that correctly?"

(By now, I'm sure you're able to compose your own three alternative questions!)

If you haven't understood them correctly, well, this is a good opportunity for them to change that.

I never cease to be amazed at the strange phenomenon of *parallel-world meetings*. Two people can leave a room, with a completely different understanding of what was discussed and agreed. In my experience, it really does happen more frequently than not.

Asked without haste, the Partnership Question will help to avoid that trap.

That's it!

Instead of depending upon your ability to persuade, impress, display your technical expertise or give clever presentations...

You now have the coherent framework of Superb Questions that was promised.

One thing to be clear about: this is a conversation not a single meeting.

There's no need to panic about cramming all seven Superb Questions into one discussion. Indeed, I regularly allow two or three phone or face-to-face meetings to cover all of those questions.

Having said that, you might be one step ahead of me, and are already wondering how to conclude each of those separate 'meetings'. So, let me ease your mind about that right now.

When I feel that attention spans are wandering, and energy levels are falling, I ask the following two questions:

1. *"Please could you summarise today's conversation from your point of view. What important items do you recall discussing?"*

When they've listed all the points they remember, I then ask them this:

2. *"And, of all that we've discussed... what has been the single most helpful point for you?"*

I try to ask these two questions at the end of every single meeting.

Never summarise the conversation yourself! If you listen carefully, you'll be invariably surprised by how different their views and feelings about the meeting are to your own.

What *you* think at this stage is of little consequence.
What *they* think is the key to how effective your questions have been.

The Thinking Bench

Sarah's dilemma wasn't unusual. She was a support manager in a financial planning firm, spinning far too many plates. She was running out of time every day. Her to-do list just kept growing.

Having developed competence and confidence over a number of years, she was now questioning her ability and worth to the growing team.

The temptation might have been for me to approach this as a time-management exercise. But I sensed the problem was deeper than that.

The truth was, this tiny lifestyle practice was trying to quadruple in size and was struggling to find a way of working that could cope with scaling up to a proper business. It's a typical story in the financial planning community.

After two hours, and one or two gentle questions from me, the problem finally emerged: *"I think my MD doesn't see me as capable of this new role,"* Sarah said.

As she spoke, emotions were painfully close to the surface. So, I helped her to construct a question that I've found helps to remove assumptions which, though *possibly* true, are unhelpful and impeding.

The question sounded like this:

"If I knew that my MD would see me as being more than capable of this new role... what would change for me?"

What flowed from Sarah, after asking herself that question out loud, completely changed the nature of the problem.

She saw that her plate-spinning was the result of a financially-successful business model that was completely inappropriate for the future the firm was striving for.

She saw that she was more than capable, as long as the business model was redesigned.

She went away excited and ready to create the prototype of a new team structure that would demand detailed discussion with her MD.

I could have done what most financial planners love to do: give way to my fix-it and persuade-them addiction; leap in with advice or a solution.

None of that would have helped Sarah. In her supremely intelligent mind lay – hidden and cowering – the causes as well as the exhausting symptoms.

My responsibility was to give her the space and ask her the simple questions that would allow her to illuminate the real problem and seek a real solution. I just had to be patient and quieten my own ego.

Combining coaching with financial planning – creating life planning – is far more than the development of skills in using certain 'tips and techniques'.

It's a mindset; it's a way of seeing the world; it's a way of being.

To become like this... to develop this **Power**... requires us to change the world we have already created with our own habits.

It requires us to practise and apply something new.

It requires us to relinquish the faith-sapping stories about *What Won't Work Here.*

And the day arrives when asking courageous, mind-shifting, memorable questions, accompanied by Brilliant Listening, becomes part of our new perspective, thinking and behaviour.

What Have You Learned?

→ In what ways does the **Power** framework of Seven Superb Questions differ from the conversation you have with potential and new clients?

→ What is the first question you tend to ask in a meeting with a new, or potential, client?

→ When was the last time you were in a client or team discussion lasting more than 30 minutes... where you never interrupted once?

→ When was the last time you were in a client meeting lasting more than 60 minutes, where you never once tried to demonstrate or discuss your Value Proposition?

→ When was the last time you conducted the first couple of client meetings, without trying to sell, persuade, convince or impress?

→ If you've constructed presentations to demonstrate just how skilled you are in your role – or to explain *"This is how we do things here"* – where would you now fit that into the **Power** framework of questions?

→ What approach and practices do you currently use – before and during the early client meetings, to create Trust?

What Will You Do Now?

→ Which of the **Power** framework questions are you going to try first? With whom? And when?

→ What would happen if you *immediately* stopped using your current presentations and explaining your so-called Value Proposition?

→ When is your next team meeting? If you're in a leadership position... how could you lead that meeting, without you trying to control or dominate? What would happen if you never once expressed an opinion or gave an instruction in that meeting?

STAGE 4

ELEVATE!

What You Need to Know About The Elevate! Stage

How I would love you to experience the sense of soaring, gliding, swooping and climbing that my clients have felt as they've eventually taken their businesses and lives to new heights, during this *Elevate!* stage.

By this stage those who've undertaken The Soul Millionaire Journey have been 'tested in the wilderness', that's for sure.

They know what it's like to step hesitatingly into the alien world of new skills and new ways of thinking – never knowing whether either would work for them.

They know what it's like to face opposition to their new-found ideas, opposition from their fears, from their team and from peers who mock what they're doing.

They know what it's like to trek through the Wilderness of doubt, minimal short-term results and a horizon that seems to be always receding.

Now, as they reach this fourth and final stage – The *Elevate!* stage – they have one more mighty battle to face.

And it's the battle with their own history, the habits and culture that they've created – and their lack of faith that they can change.

To quote the American comic strip character Pogo: *"We have met the enemy and he is us."*

The Seven Fruits of Elevation

Is it really possible that those clients could:

1. *Elevate!* their revenue and personal income?
2. *Elevate!* the trust, engagement and satisfaction that clients experience when working with them and their team?
3. *Elevate!* the influence, impact and fulfilment they feel in their revised professional role?
4. *Elevate!* their team's skills, so that excellence and extraordinary expertise permeate to the most junior levels of the firm?
5. *Elevate!* their leadership skills, so that their team feel a real sense of joy in the Why, What, How and Who of their work?
6. *Elevate!* the freedom they win to enjoy a richer life, as their business becomes more sustainable without the need for their own hectic, all-consuming involvement?
7. *Elevate!* the legacy they leave behind in this world?

Yes, it is entirely possible – nay, probable!

Seeing my clients cast off the burden of years of unhelpful habits...
Seeing them vanquish their own doubts during this battle...
Seeing them emerge as victors...

Now, that is worth all of their travails and buffeting in the chaotic storms of business, so that I can bring you these examples, this direction, this way of thinking.

With these, you can achieve the same outcomes in your world.

THE FLIGHT OF THE SOUL MILLIONAIRE

First, Focus on Elevating These Two Business Capacities

There will be time, in other books, to take each of those Seven Fruits of Elevation and expand upon them. Right now, I want to help you see how others have soared higher by distilling just two business capacities: the two roots from which those Seven Fruits are nourished:

The Two Roots

1. **Elevating** the business culture they're creating, by changing the person they're becoming.
2. **Elevating** leadership skills to create a culture of joy.

Whether it's just you and an administrator, or whether you're leading a 50-person enterprise, only effective leadership can provide the leverage you need to develop a business that can take flight.

Keep this in mind

As context, it's worth remembering the last two stages of the original eight-stage Hero's Journey:

Stage 7: The Final Test
The Hero goes through a final pivotal experience that completely transforms him.

In some stories our Hero actually dies. (Oh dear!)

However, through this death, our Hero is brought back to life as a more powerful, awe-inspiring being. He becomes someone who commands respect, even reverence, as a result of this test.

Our Hero then heads home, having cast off his old self – this time with a treasure, an elixir, or some new symbol of power.

In our Soul Millionaire Journey, we call this the stage of 'Prosperity'.

Stage 8: The New Mission

Our Hero arrives at the place he has longed for throughout his many months and adventures. This is what he aspired to.

But something has changed: our Hero can no longer go back to who he was.

In addition, something feels unfinished. In spite of all that has been won and achieved... something's still missing.

In our Soul Millionaire Journey, we call this the stage of 'Posterity'.

What *Prosperity* and *Posterity* look like will unfold before you as you study and apply this *Elevate!* stage.

I'll be right beside you as you drive forward, raising your arms and lifting your sight.

And as you start to soar.

Chapter 14

Prosperity: Through The Person You're Becoming

Now we dispel the myths and free business leaders from the monster that has engulfed them.

Now we see why the pursuit of success is frequently counter-productive. And why that success is sweeter, and enjoyed more, when you're concentrating on something else entirely.

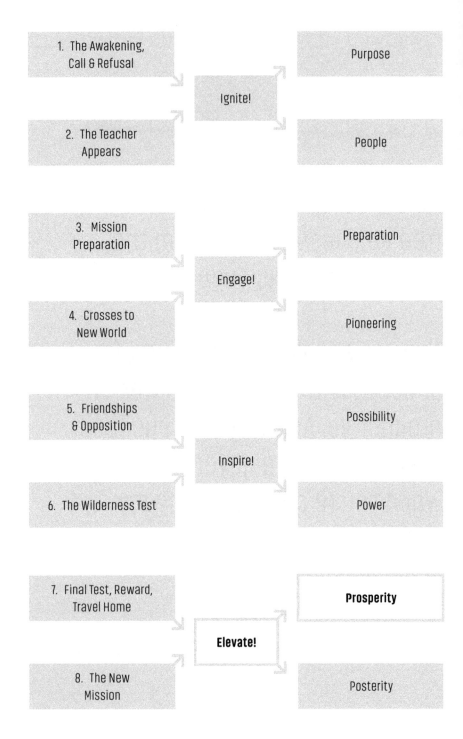

Time to Hear The Birds Sing

I picked up the phone, more irritated than expectant.
If a phone call wasn't in my diary it usually meant an automated sales interruption.

It was Alan. I could detect strange, entrancing sounds as a background to his particularly chirpy voice.

"Hello, Alan," I said, curious. *"What can I do for you? Is something wrong?"*

"Oh, hello, Dave," he responded brightly. *"No. Nothing wrong. In fact, everything is wonderfully right."*

"Well, it's good to hear from you. But where exactly are you? I can hear birdsong."

"That's right!" He was sounding downright delighted. *"We're in the New Forest – one of my wife's favourite places."*

Now I was confused. *"But, Alan, it's Friday. What are you doing in the New Forest on Friday, when you said you had so much to cope with in the office?"*

"Well..." Now it was his turn to sound confused. *"I thought you said in our coaching session that dating my wife every Friday would help to solve my problems?"*

"Oh no, no, no!" Now I was laughing. *"I meant, make a commitment to date your wife every Friday **night**. Friday **night** – not all day every Friday!"*

"Oh, right!" He chuckled. *"Well, whatever. We're having a brilliant time. And, more than that, we're falling in love all over again. I'd forgotten how stunning a woman she is."*

I'd met Alan at an annual conference of the Personal Finance Society. With hundreds of suited folk strolling around the National Exhibition Centre, in Birmingham, Alan had approached me as part of that day's Meet the Experts event: 15-minute one-on-one conversations with a coach or consultant.

Time was tight, so we got straight to the point. I asked him just two questions. The first was: *"Alan, what's on your mind?"*

After the second question, his tears welled up.

What was that second question? It's simple, actually. The question was: *"Alan, are you happy?"*

He struggled to compose himself.

I see them all the time – looking and sounding the part – directors, senior partners, founders of businesses. Strutting, looking confident; with a bag full of achievements, position and prestige, a handsome income, the house, the cars, the boat, the second home...

Yet they're discontented, empty, confused, hurting.

In Alan's case, with teenage children spreading their wings of independence, home life was stressful, to say the least.

There was friction amongst the board of directors in his company. Relationships with one or two staff weren't ideal either. Then there were those wealthy clients he wished he didn't have to see.

So started a fascinating coaching journey and the beginning of a warm friendship.

Six hours into our first face-to-face coaching meeting, I held my hand up to halt our conversation. *"Alan, I'm thoroughly enjoying this. But it's now 3:30 pm and our energy is flagging, yet we've not spoken much about your business."*

"I know." He smiled. *"Great, isn't it? Because I'm not sure right now that those problems are my priority."*

I agreed. We both felt that Alan's relationship problems at work started with his relationships at home. And with himself. So, we spent the next three months planning how to heal those.

→ **Firstly,** we agreed that he was already successful. His relentless pursuit of more and more wasn't ever going to satisfy the emptiness within.

→ **Secondly,** Alan determined that his priority was to dedicate every moment he could to demonstrating his love to each member of his family.

He committed to what we called *Dates with Dad*. One by one, each teenager could choose the place and agenda for Saturday;

THE FLIGHT OF THE SOUL MILLIONAIRE

and Alan would be with them, fully. Thoughts of business were locked away until Monday.

→ **Thirdly,** he decided to *Go to His Mountain Top* every other Friday.

I challenged him to find somewhere beautiful, peaceful, tranquil, and go regularly to that place. Nobody would be allowed to reach him on that day.

There, he would shut out all the interruptions of business and life. There he could be calm enough to receive whatever answers and inklings he needed to have revealed to him.

These weren't complex decisions. Indeed, it was their uncompromising simplicity that made them so powerful.

"Sometimes we try to run so fast that we forget where we are going and why we're running."

David A Bednar

Make A Note of What Happened

We can't have been coaching together for more than six months when Alan sent an email that has echoed in my mind ever since.

"David. There's laughter in our home again."

Now it was my turn to feel like weeping. The more we worked together, the more the positive changes rolled forth:

→ Conversations with his co-directors were becoming more positive, more empathetic, more fruitful.
→ The challenges with his staff began to be solved.
→ He released the wealthy clients, whom he found so unpleasant. Within weeks, those gaps were filled with new clients, who were equally wealthy, but noticeably less cantankerous.

I believe it was about nine months into our relationship when I asked the question that had been niggling me: *"Alan, I'm so pleased that you're enjoying these changes, but I wonder whether you've seen any measurable, monetary impact in the business, as a result?"*

"Oh," he piped up. *"Didn't I tell you? We've just had the best quarter in the history of our business!"*

With that question satisfied, I asked him the more difficult question: *"Alan, what do you think has been the underlying cause of these results?"*

I waited.

"To be honest, David," he replied, his voice breaking, *"I think it was me. I was the source of the problems. So, I had to change, and be the cause of the solutions. It was me."*

Not every man would have the courage to make that statement. But he was right.

> People – the sustaining force of our business – notice that improved wellbeing. They enjoy its proximity. They respond positively to its influence.

First Lesson: Strip Away The Rationalisations

Let's examine what Alan did, and why each change was so effective.

His first discovery was that he was chasing business growth at the expense of time and energy with those he loved most. The paradox was, both were getting diminishing returns from his efforts. Even when he was at home, he was hardly his best self.

Like too many of us, he had devoted his time in business to the undisciplined pursuit of more and more.

Couple this with fleeting accolades of praise, and the chocolate-high episodes of 'winning' and you have an intoxicating brew.

He had also bought into the illusion of *harder, faster, smarter and more* as a response to not feeling satisfied. Unbridled galloping down that road leads to stress, mechanical thinking, and, eventually, being less commercially effective.

It's also a sop to support one of the most widely used fabrications... *"I'm doing this for us, honey/kids,"* is a rationalisation that never welcomes close examination.

Yes, there are times in business when we must invest unusual hours to win or survive. Perhaps we put in a metaphorical, or real, all-nighter. But, it's when the exception becomes the addictive rule that our peace of mind and relationships start to unravel.

That addiction pulls us, siren-like, over an invisible line where *soaring* shifts to *spinning*, and then to *surviving*.

One cause of such addiction, in particular, comes to mind.

I'm still surprised at the number of business leaders who struggle to compose themselves when I ask why they're driving themselves so relentlessly. Since they're already financially comfortable, I ask: *"What's going on?"*

We peel back the past. There we find a child trying to prove themselves worthy of a parent – usually their father; a parent who was persistently absent because of business.

What's heartbreaking is that this draining habit can continue... even when their parent died years ago. Yet, here they are, in danger of leaving precisely the same legacy for their own children.

It's true. Sometimes we try to run so fast that we may forget where we are going and why we are running. We become victim to two errors of judgment that gnaw at the fabric of our lives:

1. We are confused about our priorities in life.
2. We have no clarity of **Purpose**.

Oh, we might think we know what we want. We might confuse *purpose* with *goals* and *objectives.* But the **Purpose** we think we have is actually founded on that which is transient, ephemeral and proximate. Approval. Popularity. Prestige. Position. Possessions.

When that confusion takes hold of us, emptiness follows, as sure as night follows day. So, we run harder and faster to try to fill the emptiness. Rather like the *hair of the dog.*

No. The *harder, faster, smarter and more* mentality doesn't deliver the emotional goods.

Certainty of priorities and clarity of Purpose together replace *harder, faster, smarter and more.*

That's the first lesson I relearned from Alan's story.

> There's no point trying to help an executive to change their thinking when they're sitting in the place where years of unhelpful mental habits have been formed.

Second Lesson: Be Whole, Be You

In our conversations, Alan came to recognise that he, like most of us, is a terrible actor. He'd definitely lose at poker. Try as he might, he couldn't hide from one part of his life what was going on in the other.

Frequently, we behave as if we're two separate beings. We think that if the personal element of our life is hanging by a thread then this won't affect how we perform in business. Or at least we can still act our way blithely through the day.

How blind can we be! It takes an extraordinary person to fulfil that act for any period of time. As Andrew, my former mentor, said to me, *"David, you're not a segmented orange. You're a whole peach of a human being."*

Perhaps not the most academically formidable of comments, but wise and true nonetheless.

My eyes were opened to the fantasy we create for ourselves when, in my role as leadership coach I sought help from a firm of occupational psychologists. I needed guidance and psychometric tools from them, as I reviewed the leadership potential within a number of client companies.

I learned that on average, more than 80 percent of executive behavioural traits play out both at home and at work. In other words, we are who we are, wherever we are. Each week, we bring ourselves, and our emotional rucksack, into our business. And vice versa.

Pretending that clients and colleagues can't tell we're coping with pain, heartache and contention elsewhere, is to say that everyone else is naïve, lacks insight and is socio-emotionally blind. Maybe they can't immediately tell why something doesn't *smell* right when they meet with you. But they smell it nonetheless.

Consequently, investing time and energy in our physical, mental and emotional wellbeing – including our relationships outside of work – invariably washes back as improved performance within it.

People – the sustaining force of our business – notice that improved wellbeing. They enjoy its proximity. They respond positively to its influence.

The same is true for our integrity and our intent.

Since *integrity* means *to be whole,* if we deceive in relationships within or outside of the office and then declare *"honesty is us"* in our marketing… that's an interesting, and corrosive, exercise in hypocrisy.

Eventually, the truth of who we are will reveal itself.

Before investing more effort in *fixing* your clients or your team… do your own inner work. Take steps to heal what's hurting.

That's the second lesson I relearned from Alan's story.

> He has finally realised that, when our habits lead us to work by sheer discipline, driven largely by goal-seeking forces (**harder, faster, smarter and more**) we can find the joy squeezed out of our work.

Third Lesson: Find Your Mountain Top

A common delusion in business is to assume that filling our day with worthy goal-based activity equates to productivity and superior performance. We look to heroic models of productivity around us and proclaim ourselves to be *as busy as a bee.*

The interesting fact is that bees know when *not* to be busy. They seem better wired than we are at knowing when to take time off. Even on good days, worker bees may spend up to half their day quietly patrolling the hive or resting.

It's because of this collective wisdom that they're so productive when we do see them. We could learn a thing or two from their society.

Finding your Mountain Top is part of reversing The Busy-Bee Habit. It's part of the business of thinking clearly.

One thing that is clear is that business today needs more clear-thinking from all of us. To help my new clients enjoy this better quality of thinking, I set a simple, non-negotiable protocol in my work. They need to get *off-territory* for our coaching to start.

Why do I insist on that practice?

Well, nobody would argue with the fact that our environment has a deep impact on both how well we think and what we think about. Knowing that, there's no point in me trying to help an executive to change their thinking if they're sitting in a place where years of unhelpful mental habits have been formed.

The first thing we need to do is to get them away from the place of those habits. We need to eliminate the influences that got them to where they are today.

Then there's the problem of noise.

That's another factor that needs eliminating if the best ideas are to blossom and flourish. Unfortunately... the wonder of technology provides too many opportunities to be distracted by the constant noise of the world.

If you're to think differently, that smartphone hermetically sealed to your palm is the last thing you need. The noise of life – the insistent babble and opinions of others pouring from such instruments – shreds our ability to be anything more than reactive and habitual in our decisions.

Our creativity, innovation and insight suffer as a result. So, eliminate that technology noise too. As often as you can.

Getting back to the subject of Mountain Tops...

It intrigues me that wisdom literature – from whatever philosophy or religion – speaks of prophets and spiritual leaders seeking mountains and other elevated places for their meditation. In the stories told of their lives, they return from such places with new wisdom to share with the world. A classic example is Moses returning from Mount Sinai with the Ten Commandments.

Which is why I request each client to: *"Find your Mountain Top. Then go there regularly."*

Alan reports that many of the best ideas and decisions regarding his business have come during that Mountain Top time. Every other Friday, he eliminates the possibility of interruptions and the distractions of others' urgencies.

He sits, quietly, with pen and notepad at hand. And he thinks. Then, as if by magic, into the quiet receptacle of his mind flow ideas – unbidden, unforced, unplanned – ideas that sometimes take him by surprise.

He has finally realised that, when our habits lead us to work by sheer discipline, driven largely by goal-seeking forces (*harder, faster, smarter and more*) we can find the joy squeezed out of our work.

So then... go to your Mountain Top.

That's the third lesson I relearned from Alan's story.

"Anyone can quickly and easily recognize that a joyful team will provide better outcomes."
Richard Sheridan

THE FLIGHT OF THE SOUL MILLIONAIRE

Expect This to Happen

Once Alan had seen that *he* was the problem...
Once he had made corrections in perspective, priorities and
joyless activity...

He found more than he'd anticipated flowing from these
corrections:

→   His energy was renewed.
→   His mental strength was revitalised.
→   His relationships were regenerated.

Alan's life changed because his motives had changed.

When you're in the presence of someone who is undergoing such
changes, you can't help but feel influenced by their presence. So it
was with Alan. By becoming a different person, he found that clients
and colleagues reciprocated by behaving differently towards him.

Now, some might smirk at Alan's story and the lessons I've drawn
from it. They wonder whether such personal changes can have
any impact on the business bottom line.

Why not speak to the Alans of the world? Remember:

→   Relationships with his peers improved.
→   Relationships with his team improved.
→   Irksome client relationships were solved.
→   Revenue jumped to new heights.

I've met, and worked with, many clients like Alan. The extraordinary upwards shift in the bottom line of their businesses shouts loud and clear.

Read works like *The SPEED of Trust* by Stephen M R Covey (the son of business philosopher Stephen R Covey, and the person behind the commercial success of FranklinCovey, a world leader in transforming business culture and leadership).

Stephen M R Covey's experience and success show that such social virtues – such character qualities – are hard-edged economic drivers of business. To quote him: *"Trust always affects two outcomes – speed and cost. When trust goes up, speed (of positive results) will also go up, and costs will go down. It's that simple, that real, that predictable."*

Or read *Joy, Inc.* by Richard Sheridan. He'll tell you how they created a company intentionally built on a culture with joy as its guiding principle.

Sheridan comments, *"Anyone can quickly and easily recognize that a joyful team will produce better outcomes. And (we have found) a joyful company cares deeply about the change it is making in the world."*

When you've finished reading *Joy, Inc.*, you'll understand why his company, Menlo Innovations, is visited by eager, inquisitive corporations from across the globe.

Read these books. Then try to tell me that such *soft skills* and *personal principles* like Trust and Joy are not the foundation of hard-edged, elevating commercial **Prosperity**.

You're Almost There

You're almost home.

You've travelled far, and experienced much, on this Soul Millionaire Journey.

You've been awoken from the slumber of your everyday routine.

You've found a Mission that challenged you with its scope and its unknown.

You've **Prepared**. You've stepped into a new world; a new way of thinking and doing.

You've faced opposition, possibly ridicule, and found that this came from surprisingly close to home.

Yet you've surrounded yourself with new folk: others who want to change the face of an industry, who want to **Pioneer**, just like you.

You've faced battles... and a wide, lonely wilderness of wondering whether these changes would ever make a difference.

But with grit and endurance you've sailed through those uncertain, windswept skies.

To get here, you've flown so high, soared and dived so breathlessly.

In doing so, you've changed so much.

What you've done has not left you untouched.

From this altitude, this elevated position, you can see what you sought those months ago.

You're within sight of home.

Now, you face one more mighty task. One more battle, before the victory – the richness beyond elevated personal income – is yours.

Come With Me to The Thinking Bench

Wendy and Briony, my youngest daughter, were chatting lazily, under the green parasol shading our round wooden garden table.

Meanwhile, the pungent smoke from the barbecue wafted over me, as I watched Dean skilfully flip the marinated chicken, salmon and sizzling steaks.

He's not only a singer capable of tearing at your heart and drawing out a sob: Dean's pretty hot with his culinary skills too. Our youngest daughter continues to be spoiled, as he does most of the cooking for her every day.

Between us, we lightly, languidly, touched upon many things:

→ Shoes and ships and sealing-wax.
→ Their wonder at what had happened to my bee and butterfly garden in the space of just two months.
→ Dean's former lead part in Disney's musical *Aladdin,* and his recent spell of acting in a film.

Now we spoke with more attention about his role in the forthcoming musical *The King and I,* and how both Wendy and I carry deep, fond memories of our mothers taking us to see the 1956 film, starring Yul Brynner.

I started musing then about the plot and the music that I remembered.

I marvelled at how two brilliant minds – Rodgers and Hammerstein – could take the spoilt-brat, all-powerful, polygamous king and make us love his arrogant childishness anyway.

How they could weave themes of slavery, the belittling of women, the death of those close to us, the innocence of children, and wonderful, wonderful love... whilst still holding our rapt, enchanted attention.

Mere days later would see us rising to our feet, me whistling, both Wendy and I taking turns at roaring. And our aching hands clapping as hard and as furiously as our arms would allow.

The rest of the audience rising with us. First, one there. Then another over there. And, finally, the whole of the shouting, whooping London Palladium audience rose to their feet.

From the first notes of the opening overture, heads had bobbed, feet had tapped, people had mouthed the words that captivated us since childhood.

For three hours we were not in possession of our souls. We were held bound... transported... by this ridiculous, glorious story and spectacle.

As we headed home from Victoria, having attended the show's first night, three themes had already formed in my mind.

Firstly, The King, with his delusions and his fragile grasp on what-he-thinks-he-absolutely-knows, is not unlike us... entrepreneurs who start, or lead, our business.

On the one hand, what we think we know is based on assumptions, half-truths and stories we weave in our heads.

On the other, the world looks to us to do things that are so ludicrously not-doable... if we thought too hard about these we wouldn't get out of bed in the morning.

Secondly, we too often allow ourselves to be slaves.

Slaves to habits that are no longer helpful. Slaves to fears that paralyse us and hold us to comfortable routines – weekly customs that we know will at least make money but are seldom the best we're capable of.

Thirdly, we're creative beings. We don't need to let our fragile egos, our desperate need to protect our position, and our desire to always *be* right, overrule our capacity to *do* what is right and elevating to others.

Our minds and hearts are capable of soaring beyond all that.

We can do more than build our little empires, fill our bellies to bursting, satisfy every crowing appetite, clothe our backs with labels, collect our shiny stuff and protect our territory.

If we would care just a little more... we can lead a business that will bless the lives of others.

And that very act will live on, somewhere, somehow, in someone's life.

Long after the show is over.

What Have You Learned?

→　How many of your unenjoyable client relationships do you hold on to, simply because you feel financially obliged to do so?

→　If you cut your working week down to four days... what impact would that have on your business? And what empirical evidence do you have that you're unable to make that cut?

- → If your doctor said that working more than three days per week would give you a stroke... what would you do to change the way you do business?
- → Looking back at the last week in which you worked for more than 50 hours, or put yourself under enormous strain to meet a deadline... how could you have changed that by better planning?
- → Where were you (and what were you doing) when you had your three most creative, most exciting business ideas... ever? How often do you purposefully go back to that place or activity?
- → In your eagerness to achieve the next Bigger Business Target... why exactly are you doing that? Apart from buying more stuff... how will it improve your life?

What Will You Do Now?

- → What will you do now, to structure uninterrupted time for the most important people in your life... every single week?
- → What can you change in your business so that you never, never, never have to check in with your office... when you're travelling... when you're attending a conference... when you're on holiday?
- → This year... what one day will you reserve each week that will never be interrupted by business considerations... no matter what the financial cost?

Chapter 15

Prosperity: Through Elevated Leadership

Let's Talk About Changing Your World... Through Servant Leadership

Chris glanced at me briefly and smiled. Then he started to pour the teas and coffees.

Those who were new to the quarterly meeting of team leaders, in this multi-region financial planning firm, were confused. What was this managing director doing, serving our drinks? Shouldn't he be starting the meeting, and asking us to quickly get our own?

As we sat down, he looked at me more carefully this time. And smiled again. (More on Chris later.)

He knew what I believed and valued. And he'd studied enough to remember that this was the lesson that Jesus of Nazareth taught his closest followers.

After washing their feet, which were filthy with grime and sewage from the streets, Jesus had looked at them and said: **"Whosoever will be chief among you, let him be your servant."**

Servant Leadership

Servant leadership is as demanding as it is powerful.

Few leaders of businesses, both large and small, understand this. So many of us suffer in our working life, as a result. Let me explain:

→ **Servant leadership** requires equal measures of those defining qualities: courage and humility.

→ **Servant leadership** stops us using employees and clients as mere functions in satisfying our personal agenda.

→ **Servant leadership** combines selflessness with rigorous business discipline... a Heart of Gold with a Mind of Steel.

→ **Servant leadership** enables us to leave a legacy... beyond a book of clients and a wodge of recurrent revenue.

It is the antithesis to the easier – and more intellectually, emotionally and spiritually immature – *command and control* approach still so common in business today.

The beauty is you don't need to be a major shareholder in a business to practise these qualities. You don't need to build a large team of employees, or be a major shareholder, to flex your leadership muscles. This isn't about being the boss of many staff. This is about mindset. You can lead wherever you walk and work.

> This isn't about being the boss... This is about mindset. You can lead wherever you walk or work.

Because this is first about internal change: changing *you*. Only then can any external impact on your business become possible.

Learning to become a Servant Leader is an inherent part of this Soul Millionaire Journey, and an essential root from which **Prosperity** can grow.

What's more, this is no quick fix. In your lifetime, you could never learn all that you need to learn about this.

The records remark that Jesus *"went about doing good"*: healing, lifting, giving hope and vision, strength and life. With no accumulation of property, possessions, wealth nor position, he changed the world, heart by heart.

Those not inclined to spirituality and religion can look to other names that rise as giants in our more recent history:

→ Mahatma Gandhi
→ Mother Teresa
→ Nelson Mandela
→ Emmeline Pankhurst
→ Martin Luther King Jr.
→ Benazir Bhutto
→ Malala Yousafzai
→ (I'm sure you could name many more)

These mere mortals changed their world, and our belief in what is possible. They did so by demonstrating the **Power** of Servant Leadership.

I believe – as a Servant Leader in your business – you can do the same.

Something Has to Pass Away, to Bring This New Person to Life

Think about the examples we've used so far:

→ **In The Matrix,** Neo dies. Only when Trinity whispers her love for him does he arise, more powerful than ever before.

→ **In Harry Potter,** Harry dies. In his dying, a fragment of Voldemort's soul also dies. Only then can Voldemort's **Power** be diminished, and Harry's raised to match him in combat.

→ **In The Lord of The Rings,** Gandalf the Grey dies, to return as the more powerful Gandalf the White.
Frodo – whose wounds will never heal – leaves Middle Earth, to allow Samwise Gamgee to become the leader that The Shire needs.

→ **Nelson Mandela,** the leader of violent campaigns, 'died' in prison on Robben Island. The 18 years he spent there saw the death of his old, destructive voice against apartheid. In his place rose a man capable of changing the attitudes, and future, of a nation of 41 million through more peaceful means.

→ **Martin Luther King Jr.** paid with his life for his fight to free American negroes from centuries of oppression and brutality. His assassination, as well as his famous marches and speeches, was instrumental in changing laws, attitudes and deep-set culture, impacting millions of his countrymen.

So it is with you, as you take flight in this step of **Prosperity.**
Old habits die hard. But, to give birth to this level of **Prosperity,** die they must.

Let's look back, to understand why.

In any business sector, there's an inspiring moment, when the world feels a jolt of energy as yet another brave entrepreneur gives birth to a new enterprise, no matter how tiny.

It's the tale of how most advisers and planners start their small lifestyle operation.
They're no longer somebody's employee – they're self-employed, self-controlled, self-directed. You may be one of those.

With creativity and charisma, flair and energy, determination and true grit... entrepreneurial souls like you can enjoy handsome personal rewards, with just one or two support staff.

In your sphere of activity, these qualities create opportunities and revenue for you, providing enough to pay your couple of supporters. You're the irrepressible revenue creator.

This lifestyle business you've created can work happily for many years.

> They forget that their team needs to become their priority client; that great service is founded on the nurturing of great people.

The problem starts when you, the revenue creator, decide to surround yourself with ever more bright, capable people: a real team. Unfortunately, the tendency is to continue leading in the way you did to *"get this thing off the ground"*.

This is when founder leaders become trapped by the story of their own success. They may remain blissfully unaware that their self-employed model needs to cross a threshold to morph into a small-business model.

They confuse being technically excellent, and having a profitable book of clients, with running a business that has a life of its own – independent of them.

They forget that their team needs to become their priority client; that great service is founded on the nurturing of great people.

This mistake is more common than rare.

To make the change that's needed, to win the prize that awaits, old habits and mindsets must die. On The Soul Millionaire Journey, we've already seen the need for the following mindsets to be laid to rest:

→ Historical ways of advising, with the focus on implementing financial products.
→ Old ways of defining Value.
→ The decades-old, illogical thinking in how you're paid for your services.
→ What you thought you knew about how to best engage your clients.

Now, in this step I call *Prosperity,* I'm pointing to old perspectives and habits of leadership that also need to be laid to rest. Only then can a more powerful and relevant leader arise – someone who can lift the business and take it to new heights.

I believe the Servant Leader is that more powerful person.

What Does Servant Leadership Look Like?

I wish I had learned about this superior behaviour in a different way.

It wasn't until I'd witnessed too many examples of ineffective, dysfunctional – even harmful – leadership that I began to understand how blessed I had been. As an employee, and in my Christian ministry, I had been the beneficiary of this more enlightened, mature and effective approach to life.

In business, I first took note of it when observing Chris.

Never before had I so closely observed a leader coaching and serving in a commercial context. Over a period of 12 years, he only grew more able.

Fifteen years after leaving his influence, I can share with you what will lead you towards this ideal – and what will drag you away.

I urge you to ponder the following seven habits...
Then determine, with all your resolve, to do precisely the opposite.

Do that, and you'll have created the foundation of something quite extraordinary and sustainable around you.

> *"Every single employee is someone's son or someone's daughter. Like a parent, a leader of a company is responsible for their precious lives."*
> **Bob Chapman**

The Seven Habits of Highly Ineffective Leaders

Take a look at this set of traits and then go out there and do the exact opposite:

#1: The Genius-Mindset Habit

This is the most widespread leadership habit. It's also known as *The Genius With 1,000 Little Helpers.*

It stems from a cottage industry culture, where the historical business model is not a business at all, but a self-employed, lifestyle firm.

The excitement, direction, decisions, opportunities, relationships, new clients, new revenue... they all funnel through the Genius.

PROSPERITY: THROUGH ELEVATED LEADERSHIP

The Genius doesn't feel a need to develop a superb team who can lead and manage. All the Genius needs is a small army of *skilled little helpers* to carry out his brilliant ideas.

Hilarious as my wife thinks it is... the film *Despicable Me* is a classic portrayal of this mentality.

Nobody, least of all the Genius' team of financial planners, is sure how this leader wins new high-quality client relationships. Or creates so much revenue.

In effect, the other planners in the team remain as *sweepers,* picking up the work that the leader simply doesn't have time (or the desire) to handle.

This business is built on the shifting sands of personality; it's not sustainable, replicable or scalable.

The saddest reflection of the culture created by such a leader, occurs when team members actually believe: *"Well, they can do what they want. It's their company after all!"*

#2: The Seat-of-the-Pants Habit

Ask this leader's team for a 12-month or 3-year business plan, and they'll look at you with a smile of either embarrassment or pity.

Business by bumble is a phrase I've heard to describe this habit. I wish I'd invented it. Nonetheless, I'm certainly going to share it.

Apart from accurate financial records, and some vague to-the-next-level aspirations... nobody has a clue where this leader is heading.

#3: The Avoid-Tough-Decisions Habit

One of the best ways of not breaking a promise... is to avoid making one in the first place.

This leader finds it easier not to confront difficult decisions or relationships.
Those can skilfully be put off for weeks, months and even years.

They are such adroit communicators that members of their team can leave meetings feeling vaguely satisfied, even inspired. But no one can quite recall what the leader committed to do about the ideas discussed. If anything at all.

When new employees join such a culture, it's not long before they recognise that much-needed changes might come about. But then again, they might not.

In the end, a delayed problem festers, and becomes so intense that the leader's hand is forced. Meanwhile, the team sighs at a decision made today that was glaringly obvious 12 months previously.

#4: The Befuddled-Delegation Habit

Driven by a combination of both fear and pride... this leader finds it difficult to let go.

Whether consciously done or not, the leader stifles the ambitions of team members. Those ambitions are swamped by the daily volume of *stuff* flowing from the leader's desk. The team is left choking on the flotsam.

Then there's the reverse of this habit.

The leader confuses *dumping* and abdication of responsibility with delegation. Worse, this leader confuses complexity with great client service.

Senior team members are laden with masses of responsibility... and precious little authority.

To save themselves being buried, these managers point to the need to recruit more *skilled little helpers.*

It never occurs to this leader that their complexity, and directionless pursuit of more and more and more, are the root cause of the volume of work.

So, the fixed costs (staff) inexorably increase.

And stress escalates yet another notch.

"May we ever remember that the mantle of leadership is not the cloak of comfort, but rather the robe of responsibility."

Thomas S Monson

#5: The Where-I-Get-My-Biggest-Strokes Habit

Encouraged by seemingly every conference, seminar and workshop they've attended to do only *"What You Are Best At"*, this leader has missed the point completely.

This leader swans around the country (or office) buried in as many client meetings as they can pack into a week. *"Surely I should focus on what I'm best at?"* the leader cries.

What seems to elude them is the recognition that their priority client relationship is with members of their team!

Followers need leaders to lead them.
And that requires a leader making themselves available to do so.

It's not an activity to fit between the cracks of this week's 16th and 17th client conversation on a Friday afternoon.

#6: The Dominating-Territory Habit

This leader tries so hard to encourage ideas from their team. They want their team to be *"aligned with the mission"* or *"on the same page"*.

They really do.

But they either consume the airtime in meetings by excessive talking.
Or they constantly interrupt whoever is trying to express an idea.
Or, as suggested above, they've really no intention of implementing
any ideas other than their own.

So, after decisions are discussed, they blithely, often unconsciously,
cut the legs from under their team by passive-aggressive behaviour.
They simply ignore pleas for change and ideas that aren't theirs.

Eventually, the team grows weary of putting forward ideas.
So, creativity shuts down and people do whatever is necessary to
get the job done to the best of their ability.

#7: The Busy-Bee Habit

This leader's foot is never off the accelerator.

They're not happy until they can cram another 10 new projects each
month into the hopper that's shaped like a support team.

"Time is money," they chant. So, they genuinely believe that busy-
ness equates to productivity. For them, keeping extremely busy is a
kind of opium. It allows them to ignore the bigger problems staring
them in the face.

Meanwhile, of course, lunch (and weekends) is for wimps.

The team becomes, literally, sick of the relentless waves of work being dumped onto their desk.

Stress is high. Moods are volatile. Tears are not uncommon.

Woe betide you if you're around at end-of-tax-year when stress turns to near-insanity as the leader instigates another product-focused sales fest!

These seven habits are also more common than rare.

Speaking to other coaches and consultants in various countries, it would seem that these dysfunctional leadership patterns are common amongst founder-entrepreneurs. The evidence shows they – usually unwittingly – leave a trail of hurt and confusion in their wake. Intriguingly, seldom with clients; this behaviour is largely directed at their own team.

By the time these leaders reach their late 40s and 50s, these habits can become so deeply ingrained it's a test of coaching skill to help them change.

But change they can!
Indeed, my experience is that such leaders can transform that thinking and behaviour... once they recognise and understand what is happening... why... and how things could be different.

Flip Things on Their Head

Now that you've seen how destructive ineffective business leadership can be, I'm going to take each of the Seven Habits listed above... and show you what happens when you reverse them.

Because... when we face the fact that leadership is a privilege and glorious responsibility, not a right earned by paying someone's salary...

... when we see that the minds of most teams in your business sector are capable of extraordinary ideas, creativity and invention...

... when we make our business a conduit for doing something meaningful in this world, rather than helping us to accumulate more and more...

... when we recognise that the joy – or miserable lack of it – that people feel about themselves during their 40-plus hours of work a week has a direct impact on their lives and loves at home...

Then we can reap a harvest of excellence, extraordinary service and elevated passion in the people around us, which no salary cheque or bonus can buy.

Your business can take you to heights you'll hardly recognise – if you just give it a chance.

THE FLIGHT OF THE SOUL MILLIONAIRE

The Seven Habits of The Servant Leader

Reversing Habit #1 (The Genius-Mindset Habit)

Restructure your business model, to allow the genius of others to flourish.

If your team constantly signals frustration at your behaviour... face up to it. Then you can learn new ways of behaving as a leader. Or bring someone in who can lead them instead.

If you don't know how to do either of these... ask someone who does. Or start with the study of books like *Rocket Fuel* by Gino Wickman and Mark C Winters.

Or look at the results achieved by Bob Chapman and Rajendra Sisodia in their book *Everybody Matters.* Chapman is the CEO and chairman of Barry-Wehmiller Companies and has pioneered a different approach to leadership that creates high morale, surprising creativity and business performance that's breathtaking.

How has he done that?

By reversing the *Genius With 1,000 Little Helpers* model, and by demonstrating to every single employee that their mind and heart truly matter, and that their role has real meaning.

Reversing Habit #2 (The Seat-of-The-Pants Habit)

Collaborate with your team to create a coherent, written plan for the next three years. Once that's clearly articulated, and there's a feeling of unity underpinning that three-year plan, work together on the more detailed plan for the coming 12 months. Having accomplished that together... you can plan the first 90 days of that 12 months with more **Purpose** and clearer perspective.

If the plan is as much theirs as yours, well, then there's no need to get them to *buy in* to what is agreed. They'll either be with you, or they'll decide that their future lies elsewhere.

During the course of a year, you'll probably invest four to six days in this level of planning. If well facilitated, it won't be long before you'll recognise that those days were, by a big margin, the most valuable meetings you've had all year.

Reversing Habit #3 (The Avoid-Decisions Habit)

Make a decision on tough issues. Make it now. Make a promise to those around you. Then keep your promise. Doing the opposite paralyses your business and blows your credibility.

Regularly ask yourself: *"What do I already know, that I'm going to have to face up to in 12 months?"*

Reversing Habit #4 (The Befuddled-Delegation Habit)

Ego and fear are both destructive character traits in business. As is wilful blindness to the problems we create for others.

Delegation is a learnable professional skill. It doesn't seem to come to most of us naturally, however.

Learning how to communicate the *why,* as well as the *what* and *when,* gives context to their unspoken question, *"What has this to do with the direction the firm is heading?"*

As part of your learning, be considerate and realistic. Which of the other 35 projects sitting in their inbox can they push aside, to make room for this new *massively urgent* project? A moment of clarity on your part will save their frayed nerves, costly mistakes and fractured evenings away from their families.

Meanwhile, if you'll just get out of their way – having first properly educated, trained and nurtured them – people will astound you with what they're capable of rising to.

As one such leader commented, when I asked why his firm was regularly winning industry awards, *"They've proved that they can grow to become better than me in their technical skills. My role is to become the leader they deserve."*

> "They've proved that they can grow to become better than me in their technical skills. My role is to become the leader they deserve."

Reversing Habit #5 (The Where-I-Get-My-Biggest-Strokes Habit)

Once you recruit people into your world... your role has already changed.

The only question is: *"Are you changing at the same pace?"*

If you want followers, then your primary responsibility is to stop just 'doing the job' and invest in your ability to lead.

When you've raised your team to the level they're capable of, then they'll free you to fly to heights that were never possible before.

Reversing Habit #6 (The Dominating-Territory Habit)

In meetings, recognise that others have brilliant minds too. And deep feelings. You're not the only Genius in town.

Say far less. Listen far more. Give people room to think, speak and say what needs to be said. If you feel you absolutely must speak... make sure that your intention is to ask Superb Questions. Then Listen Brilliantly, of course.

Give them permission to stop dancing around the truth. To say what needs to be said, even if it's scary or, seemingly, counter-culture.

Almost invariably, they'll surprise you.

If you really wish to create an environment where the quality of your team's ideas takes your breath away, I recommend you study and apply the principles in Nancy Kline's book, *Time To Think.*

Reversing Habit #7 (The Busy-Bee Habit)

One of my favourite Christmas gifts (apart from the birth of our youngest daughter) was an annual subscription to *National Geographic.* The depth of research conducted on global issues is astounding.

I spent a year reading about the impact of the beautiful National Parks on the wellbeing of people who spent time visiting them.

What was interesting was the *measurable* improvement in executive creativity and decision-making that resulted from three of four days in such an environment. For *measurable,* read as high as 50 percent!

When a business is horrendously busy, it's a clear sign of unconscionably poor thinking at the top.

Stressed minds, tired bodies and weary emotions revert to 'mechanical' behaviour. Under this pressure, the brain shelves creativity. Stress hormones raise blood pressure, and the heart rate increases.

PROSPERITY: THROUGH ELEVATED LEADERSHIP

When this happens, your people make more mistakes – mistakes that could prove geometrically costly to you.

So, give those minds a chance to breathe, by reviewing your behaviour, so as to release them from the mire of stuff you love to throw at them.

Perhaps the first step would be to simply stop throwing for a while!

> When a business is horrendously busy, it's a clear sign of unconscionably poor thinking at the top.

Study Causes, Before Reacting to Symptoms

It's easier to reverse the Seven Habits of Highly Ineffective Leaders when we recognise what causes the different types of thinking and behaviour.

It was Stephen R Covey who first opened my eyes to the impact of a person or business model failing to grow to the next level of maturity.

At the Business Childhood level, we practise *dependence:*

→   This is about you.
→   You're responsible for me.
→   You're to blame if something doesn't work.

→ You must make me feel safe, secure and wanted.

→ You command, and I'll obey.

→ You're the person with the **Power**; I'm just your employee.

At the Business Adolescence level, we grasp *independence*:

→ This is the typical small-firm Financial Adviser and Financial Planner model.

→ This is about me.

→ I'm accountable to nobody but me.

→ I seek high income, achievement and status.

→ I'm the Genius, and you're my little helpers.

→ I must compete and win, externally and within the business.

→ I hold the reins of **Power**.

At the Business Adulthood level, we awaken to *interdependence*:

→ This is about *us.*

→ We seek more than money and status: we seek work with Meaning and **Purpose**.

→ We're both accountable and responsible to each other and our mission.

→ We don't compete with each other; we enjoy the multiplying effect of collaboration.

→ Our combined ideas make the *what* and *how* of our business easier and more influential.

→ Unified we're more powerful than working on separate agendas.

What's clear is that Business Adulthood is far more rare than common.

Decades ago, Neil Sedaka sang that *"Breaking up is hard to do"*.
So – as my perceptive wife, Wendy, points out to me – is growing up!

Meanwhile... You Really Can Lead From The Bottom Up

I remember facilitating a Quarterly Strategy Day with a team of directors.
For various reasons, Anna, a more junior member of the team, was invited.

I hadn't briefed her properly. So, it soon became clear that she assumed her presence was desired to observe and take notes.

Quickly, I changed her assumption, and she became part of the discussion.

Within an hour, it was clear to all of us that Anna's bright mind was superseded only by her piercing insight. She succinctly summarised things that we had been dancing around all morning.

You could have been fooled by her hesitation and sweet, gentle, timid voice.
But we knew we were facing a force to be reckoned with.

The MD could see what was happening, and eventually – with some guidance and persuasion – got out of the way of her thinking and talking.

Within four years, this bright young thing, Anna, became the Chief Executive of the company!

She just needed others to step aside, stop using her back to *shift stuff,* and let her spread her wings.

Everybody in Anna's team agrees that the future looks brighter than ever.

> *"This [kind of leading] requires another kind of learning, a learning that helps us forget what we know and discover what we need."*
>
> **Robert Quinn**

If you change your perspective and behaviour in even one of these Seven Habits...

... if you'll harness the collective **Power** of your team's minds and hearts

... you'll find that this **Power**, this team you've gathered around you, can move mountains.

Or they can be the wind beneath your wings.

The Thinking Bench

I had recently been ill for nearly three weeks. Weak. Weary. Wobbly.

And here I was, slowly clambering around the hills and mountains of the Lake District. Clearly, I was slightly mad.

My guide, Richard, had treated me gently on the first day. A ramble over hillsides of bluebells and gorse. The sounds of little waterfalls. Lovely.

But here – on the third day – my body was screaming, after four hours of striding and scrambling up the 2,900 feet that is Great Gable. All I could think of was where to put my foot next without breaking my ankles.

But at the summit, standing atop a cairn of grey rocks.
The stunning view! The colours! The elation!
I hardly dared breathe, breathless as I was. Yet I felt that I could see forever!

Oh, my word! Look where I have travelled from... and to!

We are all travellers.

The question is not whether we've travelled far. The question is only that of direction; and whether that direction takes us to a level where our perspective becomes more panoramic, less myopic.

And, in our journeying and our arriving, whether we appreciate:

→ What we have brought with us to offer to others.
→ What we have learned.
→ Who we have become.

You've arrived. This is the place.

If you've fulfilled all that The Soul Millionaire Journey has asked of you... nothing will ever be the same.

When you've applied these principles, you should find every element of your life elevated and ennobled.

If you're like the characters whose stories you've experienced, you'll feel enriched. Indeed, your revenue and income will reflect that.

Moreover, it will be easier to 'find yourself', because now, having given yourself to nurturing others, there's more of you to find.

You've journeyed and flown where few of your industry have ventured.

You've **Pioneered** where others can follow, if they dare.

The business you've helped to craft is a delight to lead... exciting to work for... transformative for clients to engage with.

You should feel good about yourself. Thoroughly satisfied.

However...

it's probable that you don't.

Because although you've reached 'here' – the place you dreamed of – something remains unfinished.

It's that 'something' that can only be addressed when you've created a legacy beyond money, beyond revenue, assets and personal wealth.

Let's create that legacy.

1299.

What Have You Learned?

→ How would you describe your leadership style today?

→ How do you think others speak about your leadership behaviour?

→ Where do you believe you are on the spectrum moving from Business Adolescence to Business Adulthood?

→ How unpleasantly busy would you describe your typical week? How busy and stressed do you cause other people to be?

→ If a leadership coach were to review your leadership qualities in three years' time... What would you like them to say about the three specific areas in which you've improved?

→ When was the last time your business invested in a leadership course for you? For other members of your team?

→ As you consider the leaders you have worked for, or observed, which of the Seven Habits of Highly Ineffective Leaders have you seen most clearly and regularly manifested?

→ Can you name one leader you personally know who demonstrates at least three of the characteristics under the *Seven Habits of The Servant Leader* section?

What Will You Do Now?

→   If you were to pick three leadership strengths you'd like
    to develop... which would you choose?
→   What would stop you investing in such development?
→   Would you be prepared to conduct a formal 360 review of
    your leadership... where your team are able to confidentially
    and anonymously comment on your strengths and weaknesses
    as a leader?

Chapter 16

Posterity

It's here you're faced with
the temporary nature of your
achievements, and your life.

And the opportunity you have to
leave behind an enduring mark
that helps others find their way.

It's here you see that others need
you to be more than you are today...
so that they can be so too.

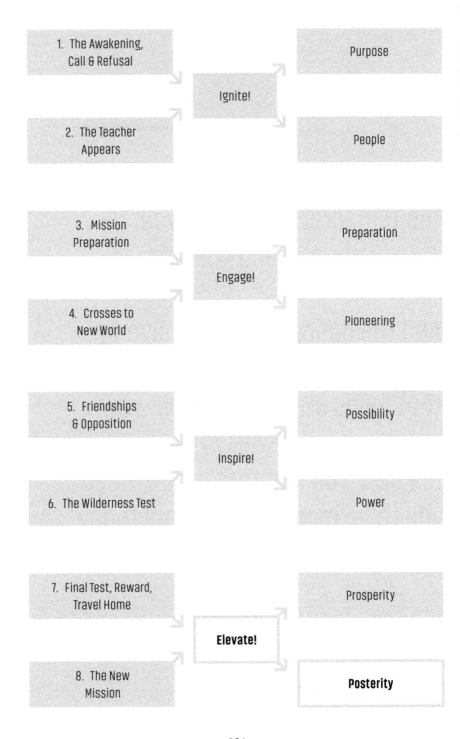

See The Princess, Watch The Prince

Our four-year-old daughter was beside herself, tugging at my jacket.

"What is it, Pumpkin?" I asked as my drink spilled over my hand.

"Daddy. The princess smiled at me!"

I followed the direction of her pointing, and there was the bride. Naturally jet-dark hair, set against a shimmering white dress. Growing up, she had always been stunning. How could she be anything else but a princess?

We were in the grounds of what could only be described as a mansion. It was to become the setting for my first book *The Soul Millionaire.* The day was hypnotically English Summer.

The groom looked every bit as exotic as the bride he had waited more than two years to marry.

This was Don. The person on whom I would eventually base a character in *The Soul Millionaire.*

A North London boy, with parents from the tiny Dutch Caribbean island of Aruba, Don loved to play jazz while Sarah loved to sing. Behind his relaxed, jovial manner was a confidence and brightness of spirit that I found magnetic.

He'd only recently returned from serving a two-year mission for his church – a mission that demanded total selflessness day and night. A mission that changed his perspective and his life.

When such missionaries return home, it's generally agreed that they've leapt 10 years or more in emotional and spiritual maturity because:

→   They're exceptional at developing deep relationships.
→   They've been constantly tested in leadership and teaching skills.
→   They understand the qualities of grit, endurance and an abiding hope when they're away from home comforts in challenging, alien situations.

Bring those factors together, and it's not surprising that The Princess had found her Prince.

In his career, Don became a much-loved and inspiring teacher.

He then tried his hand at corporate life and developed a portfolio career there, ranging from accounting to Executive Learning and Development within an HR team.

Turn The Tables

Soon after that wedding, our paths merged when our spiritual ministries brought us together.

I was responsible for developing and leading an ecclesiastical team of 12 Elders, with responsibilities covering East and West Sussex and Surrey. Don was the fresh, inquisitive junior member of that team.

A decade later, Don presided over that region, which meant that I was accountable to him. The Student had become the Teacher.

We've worked together in other ministering and leadership assignments since then. As I write, I'm still reporting to him.

More recently, our business interests began to merge. He became so interested in coaching as a career that he started to shadow me in my speaking and coaching roles.

Within a couple of years, he was developing – with enormous success – those coaching skills in his corporate HR position. He even won a professional award for his impact on changing leadership styles – and performance – within an international group.

It won't surprise you that, during a period of major change within my business, I chose to be coached by Don.

Yet again, the roles were reversed. Don helped me to examine areas of my thinking and capabilities that I had become blind to.

Embarking on this book is a direct outcome of that coaching relationship.

"Life is no 'brief candle' to me. It is a sort of 'splendid torch' which I have got hold of for the moment, and I want to make it burn as brightly as possible before handing it on to future generations."

George Bernard Shaw

All Arise

For me, this is one of the joys of nurturing and developing others, particularly in business. Not so that we may laud over them in our knowledge and wisdom, but rather so that we can create in others a greatness which builds upon our lives... and then supersedes it.

This – rather than our awards, attainments, accumulation of wealth – will mark the heritage we leave in the lives of our **Posterity**.

The way I see it, a great leader gathers around themselves those who could be capable of accomplishments greater than the leader who recruited them.

The task of that leader is to ensure that **Possibility** becomes reality. As the team rises in excellence and capacity... so does the leader.

As the Quakers would say, *"I lift thee, and thee lift me."*

In thinking once more about leading and lifting, I'd encourage you to remember that leaving this bright light of legacy has little to do with your position in a company. This legacy is more to do with your desire to leave a community, however small, rejoicing in their improvement because you lived there.

How, then, does this play out, particularly in a small business?

We're back to Servant Leadership.

If you take your attention away from 'doing the job' – the technical aspect of your work – and concentrate for a period on developing others to do that work... everybody wins.

You'll strengthen your ability to set aside the instant gratification of 'what's easiest and most obvious'.

You'll become masterful at developing the relationships that hold the greatest leverage for sustained success.

That's true leadership.

When you pay attention to Brilliant Servant Leadership– not Technical Expertise – it eventually grabs you as a dancing partner. It guides your steps, shaping what you do, and who you become.

Alternatively, you can refuse to see the **Power** of the next generation – your **Posterity**.

Or, you can blindly hoard a lifetime of wisdom and knowledge for yourself, so that you can concentrate on the client relationships that provide such self-affirming feedback for you.

Instant gratification, maybe. But it's a short-sighted decision, that's for sure.

Wake Up to The Impact of Leaving a Private Legacy

One day, perhaps after you're gone, they'll talk about you.

They'll talk about the Private Legacy you've left behind.
They'll talk about the Public Legacy that is linked to your name.

What is this 'Private Legacy'?

Well, we're certainly not talking about money in this chapter. That's too shallow an understanding of what a life can leave as an imprint, as its **Posterity**.

By 'private' I don't necessarily mean those closest to us, such as our family or our loved ones, even though I believe that these are our greatest treasures in this life.

By 'Private Legacy' I'm referring to those individuals whom our life has touched, lifted, enriched:

→ They might be our children.
→ They might be others we love and have befriended.
→ They might be members of the team we've helped to build.
→ They might be individual client relationships.

What such legacy-creators have in common is that they impact people one at a time, rather than aim to hold sway over the crowd.

As a Soul Millionaire (which is what you'll inherently become by taking this Journey), your responsibility is to see these Private Legacies as the next Heroes.

This is no longer about you, nor about your own heroic journey.

Your job is not just to be their boss. You will become the Teacher who appears 'when The Student is ready'.

You're there to wake them up.
You're there to help them see the greatness within them. To see what they hardly dare believe about themselves.

Your role is to help them see how their potential can be aligned with the Mission and Vision that fuels your company.

This is part of your private victory over the urgent need to win your own monthly accolades. Your rising above the desire to do what you do merely in pursuit of personal gain and self-aggrandisement.

This and only this should be your Private Legacy to your immediate world.

"Do you want to sell sugar water for the rest of your life, or do you want to come with me and change the world?"

**Steve Jobs, talking to
John Sculley, Head of Pepsi**

Wake Up to The Impact of Leaving a Public Legacy

What is this 'Public Legacy'?

Well, I see two possibilities here:

→   **Firstly,** the impact you have on the industry you represent, and the Posterity that will forge the future of that industry.
→   **Secondly,** the influence you have on the wider community you choose to serve.

Your impact on your industry.

I believe that each of us is accountable for the impact we make on the community that provides us with all that supports our life and lifestyle.

That community starts with the profession we've embraced. It extends to the wider community, without whom our industry wouldn't exist.

Either way, our behaviour leaves its mark.

My early efforts at this coaching and speaking career of mine were helped by generous and gracious people.

Without exception, they wore heavy mantles of responsibility, both in their businesses and in their industry. Yet they set aside time to help me in my fumbling attempts at forging a new life.

I recall leaders such as Barry Horner of Paradigm Norton; leaders who would set aside time to answer questions and submit themselves to my leadership-skills interviews.

The memory of such leaders – determined to share knowledge with their peers and bequeath their discoveries to Posterity – sits in sharp contrast to those equally determined to jealously guard so-called intellectual property in the tiny cupboards of their lives.

Yes, there are some who will parade the conference platforms in an attempt to glorify their own experience and name.

Yet, thankfully, there are more who set aside their self-interest in an attempt to lift their professional community to new heights of understanding and service.

They travel the country, dedicating precious hours and days to speaking, supporting, campaigning, planning and designing a better collective future.

For me, this is the first Public Legacy to which we should give our attention.

To give back a little to our profession, from which we have taken for years – surely this kind of legacy is not too much to ask of any of us?

Moreover, if more people would lift and inspire and show others a better way of thinking and behaving... then everybody's work and lives would be enriched. Everybody's.

We don't have to ponder too long to recognise the behaviours that history will regard with gratitude – and the names and organisations that will disappear from the footnotes of that history.

Be The One to Earn The Trust of The Wider Community

Then there is a wider community, on whom your behaviour creates ripples – whether or not you acknowledge it or are aware of it. You see, often unconsciously, you will leave a mark on the world.

What if that mark was one of increased trust?

What if the way we behave in business gave the general public reason to praise and look up to our professional community?

I contend that this is a legacy for which each of us is responsible. And we need to do something about increasing that trust, and we need to do so with a sense of urgency.

It cannot have escaped your notice that heavier regulation always follows a history of broken trust. Always. Enron, in the USA, is a perfect example of that cause and effect.

The level of new regulation and legislation that followed Enron's systemic corruption has burdened a vast array of companies with weighty layers of compliance and auditing.

And it's the same in the UK.

If you're complaining about the burden of regulation... then look for examples of broken trust somewhere in your professional community.

> Moreover, if more people would lift and inspire and show others a better way of thinking and behaving... then everybody's work and lives would be enriched. Everybody's.

How, then, can public trust be regained? And what part can we play as part of our Public Legacy?

I turn again to comments by Stephen M R Covey in his book *The SPEED of Trust.* I don't believe it's possible to read through even the first three chapters of that book without recognising that:

→   Trust is something we can do something about.
→   Creating trust is something we can become good at.

In doing so, a business creates an elevated culture throughout its fabric, and with elevated results to match. It also becomes a model that other professionals can readily follow.

Experience in other industries shows that such trust can ripple out from the individual... to the relationships within an organisation ... then to those relationships the organisation creates and touches externally... and finally to the wider market.

The challenge is knowing what components you can work on, in order to create this seemingly elusive quality, trust, within your organisation.

Covey points to four components at the heart of such trust and credibility:

1.   Integrity
2.   Intent
3.   Capabilities
4.   Results

We've spoken about all four of these, in some way, throughout this Soul Millionaire Journey. However, in brief summary, I view them in this way:

Integrity
This is about more than just being honest or telling the truth.

This is about aligning your public persona with your private reality. Being exactly who you portray yourself to be when no one is looking.

Not being duplicitous. Being integer, meaning whole or complete in Latin. Making promises. Then keeping them. So that your family speaks of you privately in the same glowing language that your business colleagues do publicly. And vice versa.

When lived, all of these facets create trust in relationships between people and communities.

Intent

If everybody knew your real agenda – the motives behind your actions – would they love what you're doing? Would they be excited about what you're advising them to do?

If your motives are essentially self-serving, do you honestly believe that the world will never see that?

If you're acting with sincerity, if you're motivated by love, compassion, a desire to lift and bless others... can you see why that will also shine through?

Capabilities

Are you still prepared to pay the price to serve better today than you did yesterday?

Are your skills, knowledge, attitude and aptitude still relevant? Is lifelong learning part of your ethos?

Results

We've heard it said many times...

After all is said and done... a lot more is said than done.

When trying to gain trust, results count. But they may not be obvious at first glance.

Yes, it might be that you can rightfully proclaim your new industry award to the market...

Or that you've found a way, which others can learn, to create just the perfect volume of Ideal Client relationships you wish to work with...

Or perhaps you've won a famous-brand new client; a name you can put on your website...

Or you've earned the right to publish a couple of testimonials, showing the excellent outcomes you helped those clients to create in their life...

Or it might simply be that you *hoed to the end of the row:* you didn't give up on a responsibility or relationship or project... even when it would have been much easier to do so. You created the result.

> This is about aligning your public persona with your private reality. Being exactly who you portray yourself to be when no one is looking.

To Covey's insights I would add one component of trust that has served me and my clients well...

Relevance

That is, developing the capacity to serve a particular segment of the community. To serve them in such a way that they appreciate the time and effort you've obviously taken to understand them.

This community senses that you care and know them... long before they meet with you.

They can see that you've invested deeply, in order to serve them in a way that few others are willing to do or are capable of doing.

Do this and people will see you as credible (and trustworthy) even before you've directly engaged with them.

> *"I am leaving this legacy to all of you...*
> *Without vision, the people will perish, and*
> *without courage and inspiration, dreams*
> *will die – the dream of freedom and peace."*
> **Rosa Parks**

Imagine what might happen if every organisation in your industry fulfilled these five criteria:

1. Integrity
2. Intent
3. Capabilities
4. Results
5. Relevance

What would happen to the way the public views your industry?

Making the question more personal:

If you knew that you could improve your industry's future by leaving an enhanced Public Legacy...

What would you do differently?

> As you look back, what matters is not just where and how you have travelled to reach here. What matters more is who you have become in that travelling.

One Last Time
Come With Me to
The Thinking Bench

It's Time Now To Look Back. And Forward

Dear Hero,

You have travelled long. You have travelled far. You have overcome.

More importantly, you've chosen – even by reading this far – a different way.

In the language of M Scott Peck, you have taken *The Road Less Traveled.*

Or as Minnie Louise Haskins would confirm, you have *"... trod gladly into the night"*. And have been led *"... towards the hills and the breaking of day in the lone East"*.

At first, I wondered what Haskins meant by that last phrase. Then I considered what my senses were telling me, and it was this:

→ Taking me *"towards the hills"* suggests leading me to a higher point in the landscape where my sight will behold a new vista, a fuller, truer, less short-sighted perspective;

→ *"The breaking of day"* suggests to me a journey from darkness to fresh new light and hope;

→ And *"in the lone East"* conjures up the same imagery as M Scott Peck describes. Few would have taken this *'Road Less Traveled'*. There would not (yet) be crowds here. Few there would be who had found this higher point in the landscape.

Because, what is better, truer and more inspired is seldom what is, at first, most popular.

So welcome, Traveller, Voyager. Welcome to the *Breaking of Day:* the dawn of the rest of your life of Possibilities.

However, before we reach the conclusion of our travelling together, I have a question; and it's this:

Did you spot the underlying message to this voyage, this Soul Millionaire Journey?

Because, like a parable, or a film (apparently created for children), the whole story of this book has layers of messages. Some readers will find their answers in the first, most visible layer. Others will find another set of messages two or three layers underneath that. Each will see what they find.

What about you?

Did you see that the emotion, the yearning, the voice whispering to you in the wind, was laid before you in the first few sentences of the Introduction to this book?

Did you see that there's one word – one – which encapsulates the beginning and the end?

Did you see?

**More importantly, did you also see this truth:
That, as you look back, what matters is not just where and how you have travelled to reach here?**

What matters more is who you have become in that travelling.

Because what we are becoming is not merely the sum total of our daily pursuits over the course of our business lifetime. Rather, it is the result of practising the humility and courage to change, when all seems perfectly comfortable and acceptable for now.

When we make that change, we'll not only have a more accomplished and richer business... we will become the catalysts in blessing the lives of others. Many of these lives we will never meet.

We will have used our education and skills to brighten those lives as opposed to only bringing benefit to ourselves and those who inherit our genes.

We will have ensured that others can take this baton we carry today and fly higher and faster tomorrow than we ever could.

And **this**... this I believe is the **Purpose** and the *summum bonum* of our work: to create something – however limited in size – whose influence is greater than our one life. To bring our dream to life, and to allow that dream to lift others.

In doing so, we will have made of our business the conduit and instrument for doing something magnificent on this earth.

This is how mankind will remember us.

This is what our name will stand for.

This – you will discover – is what is meant by being A Soul Millionaire!

FIN

Bibliography

Books

Joseph Campbell, *The Hero with a Thousand Faces*

Bob Chapman and Raj Sisodia, *Everybody Matters: The Extraordinary Power of Caring for Your People Like Family*

Jim Collins, *Good to Great: Why Some Companies Make the Leap and Other's Don't*

Jim Collins and Jerry Porras, *Built to Last: Successful Habits of Visionary Companies*

Stephen MR Covey, *The Speed of TRUST: The One Thing that Changes Everything*

Stephen R Covey, *The 7 Habits of Highly Effective People: Powerful Lessons in Personal Change*

Carol S Dweck, *Mindset: The New Psychology of Success*

Greg McKeown, *Essentialism: The Disciplined Pursuit of Less*

Steve Moeller, *Effort-less Marketing for Financial Advisors*

Nancy Kline, *Time to Think: Listening to Ignite the Human Mind*

M Scott Peck, *The Road Less Traveled: A New Psychology of Love, Traditional Values and Spiritual Growth*

Richard Sheridan, *Joy, Inc.: How We Built a Workplace People Love*

Bronnie Ware, *The Top Five Regrets of the Dying: A Life Transformed by the Dearly Departing*

Gino Wickman, *Traction: Get a Grip on Your Business*

Gino Wickman and Mark C Winters, *Rocket Fuel: The One Essential Combination That Will Get You More of What You Want from Your Business*

Bruce Wilkinson, *The Dream Giver: Following Your God-Given Destiny*

Other

Julie Littlechild and Steve Wershing, CFP® (Podcasts)

Jane Adshead-Grant (Coach)

About the Author

David J Scarlett is the founder of The Soul Millionaire leadership coaching programmes, and the creator of the revolutionary business concept The Soul Millionaire Journey.

Working with boutique firms in the financial planning community, David helps leaders and executives create iconic organisations, lead exceptional teams, live the lives they'd really love... and ultimately make a greater difference in their world.

David's first book, *The Soul Millionaire,* was an Amazon Best Seller and introduced a fresh perspective to the impact of business and money on our lives.

The parable was based on David's life where, age 28, he was broke, homeless and desperate.

David then turned his life around, repaid over £100,000 of debt, and became a respected fee-based financial planner and, eventually, an executive coach. His story has influenced many entrepreneurs across the world.

This new book takes the ageless principles underpinning his original book *The Soul Millionaire...* and maps them into any small to medium size business, transforming the way they think, impact others and accomplish surprising performance and results.

Immerse yourself in the Journey.

Just make sure you're ready for the transformation you're about to experience!

soulmillionaire.com
david@soulmillionaire.com